To Ryan —
Hope you are still
having fun with chess!
Best wishes,
Coach Ron — *9/14/14*

Chess Handbook
for Parents and Coaches

Ronn Munsterman

United States Chess Federation Certified Coach

Happy Early Birthday!

Published by Createspace – a member of the Amazon group of companies.

Munsterman, Ronn.
Chess Handbook for Parents and Coaches / Ronn Munsterman

www.ronnmunsterman.com
Read Ronn's Chess Blog: http://ronnmunsterman.blogspot.com/
Twitter Ronn: @CoachRonn

The chess diagrams in this book were created with Chessdiagrammer Version 5.2, by permission, Ekkehard May. www.chessdiagrammer.com

Manufactured in the United States of America
10 9 8 7 6 5

ISBN 1-451-57625-0

For

Berta
wife and love of my life.
Family
Stefanie, Nathan, Alexandria, Eric, Julia, and Jessica

I love you all.

Acknowledgments

The idea for this book came from my wife and best friend, Berta. Her encouragement was key to this book being what it is. Berta, thanks for a fine job of editing. You keep me from wandering too far off the path "now and then."

To my first readers: John Skelton, my friend, high school buddy, and chess club cohort; my son, Nathan; and my friends Derek Williams and Mike Holmstedt. Thanks to each of you, the book is better.

Cover Photo: Ronn Munsterman
Checkmate Pattern 1 – Queen and Knight

Back Cover Photo: Ronn Munsterman
Of Nathan Munsterman

Contents

Introduction

What this book does for you, the parent or coach

Kids are drawn to chess; they can't help themselves. Place the pieces on a board in an elementary school setting and the kids will flock to you. They love to watch someone play. They love to touch the pieces. The feel of them, the weight, the beauty, all call to them.

Whether you're a chess player yourself, or are new to chess, this book will help you teach your child how to play chess. We start with the basics. The lessons are the same ones I used while coaching elementary and then later, as my players grew older, high school students. Based on the repeated success of my students in scholastic tournaments, this teaching program passed with flying colors (See About the Author). Each lesson is laid out in bite-sized nuggets, which makes it easier for you to judge how your child is soaking up the information, and simplifies things so he grasps it quickly, and most importantly, so both of you have a lot of fun.

May I repeat that last part? So you and your child have a lot of fun. Chess players (the adult ones) often discuss aspects of chess that I like to call its nebulous factor: is it science or art? Is it a game or a sport? Ask kids the same questions and they'll look at you with a "huh?" expression. Like, what's the point of that? To young players, it's a game and it's fun. It's just that simple. We shouldn't complicate things.

Whether a parent wants to teach chess or find a coach instead, this book gives everyone insights into the game, and the world of chess, including tournaments, and answers the questions many people ask.

I lay out the minimum requirements for a player to play in a tournament and this information will help you determine when your player is ready, if that's something you and he decide to do.

I'll give you, the teacher, what you need to know and what your student needs to know in each lesson.

Not only will I present the information for you to give to your child, I'll give you some tips on how to explain it.

My kid play chess? You're kidding, right?

Depending on your child's age, if you ask whether he would like to learn to play chess, you may get a "Huh?" or a shrug, or an "Oh, I guess," and if you're really lucky, an eye roll.

In an age where our children's attention is pulled first one way then another through their activities, as well as Wii, Play Station, X-box, and PC games, it's a wonder they can keep up with anything. Not to mention the challenges *you* face as their chauffeur and administrative assistant, and yet remain the parent.

The question isn't always whether they want to play, but how you can entice them to try it. One thing you might try is to get the movie *Searching for Bobby Fischer*, which tells the true story of Josh Waitzkin. At the age of seven, Josh began playing chess, and I won't give away the story except to say that he's now an adult and is ranked as an International Master (just below Grandmaster). Josh is a terrific young man, and when my son, Nathan, played in the 2001 Supernationals, held in Kansas City, Nathan got to speak to Josh for a few minutes while getting his autograph. Josh has a ready and quick smile, and is wonderfully friendly. Not your stereotypical chess player.

What do I mean by that remark? Chess isn't just for geeks, nerds, or whatever labels folks like to assign to people who choose to exercise their mind. Chess appeals to people of all ages, genders, and professions. I've played tournament games against truck drivers, doctors, lawyers, ministers, accountants, government employees, computer programmers, teachers, PhDs, and high school drop outs. I could go on and on, but I think you get the idea.

Nowadays, students are rarely known by one label, the jock, the honor student, the artist, the geek. They are well-rounded. Today's young people are busy. They have lots of activities, some think too many, but that's a topic best discussed elsewhere. It has been my experience, and I know of other coaches who've had similar experiences, while coaching chess for elementary and high school students, that chess was only a part of these young people's lives. Many played sports; baseball, football, basketball, and were starters on their teams. Many were good students, some outstanding, others struggled in school, but all loved chess.

Some of the things about chess that attract people are its logic, purity, and variability. No two games are exactly the same. The permutations of chess are staggering. If you're interested in numbers, the number of possible positions is somewhere on the order of 10^{50}, or a ten followed by fifty zeroes. If you wrote the number one on the goal line of a football field, and wrote a zero on each yard line going toward the other goal line, the last zero would be on the fifty yard line! I don't know about you, but this is a number just too big for me to imagine. In reality, though, there are plenty of games that start out exactly the same, and then one of the players makes a move that is called a variation, which is like taking the left fork in the road instead of the right, and the game takes on a completely different path and tone.

Chess is a wonderful game. It pits one person's mind against another's. Teaching your child or a team of players to play the game well is a rewarding experience. No matter how well you yourself play the game, teaching the game to someone else can seem daunting, but that's what this book is for. It will give you the tools and guidance to not only teach children how to play the game, but to have fun at the same time.

Teach Chess? Who me? Yes you!

Regardless of your child's age, you *are* a teacher. You teach your child daily, sometimes directly by showing or telling him or her something new, or indirectly as a result of your example.

If you can play chess, you can teach it to your child by following the lessons. If you don't know how to play, I recommend that you read each lesson first by yourself and play through any exercises. Then, when you're comfortable with the material and by following the instructions as presented, you can teach your child. In either case, this book has you covered!

An aside to chess coaches

Perhaps you've been coaching awhile, or you're thinking about starting a chess club or program. Perhaps you teach at a school. Maybe you want to volunteer at the school your child attends. Everything in this book applies to teaching a group of children to play chess, after all, that's how these lessons came to be. All of the information about tournaments will help you prepare your chess team to compete. Chapters 5 and 6 are written especially for coaches and include lots of coaching tips and a section called Funner Games, some of which are well-known in the chess world, and others I just made up, more or less on the fly, that kids love to play. These games are ideally suited to club time.

This book's structure

This book is divided into two parts: Part One – Teaching Chess, and Part Two – The Chess World. The chess lessons are in Part One and each is titled Lesson "number." Information about the chess world: tournaments, chess organizations, chess clubs, and coaching, is in Part Two and each is titled Chapter "number."

Benefits of playing chess

There are many analysis papers and articles on the benefits of playing chess. If you do an internet search for "benefits of chess," you'll find an enormous number of articles.

The New York City Chess-in-the-schools program (www.chessintheschools.org), which has been around for over twenty years, provides chess instruction for elementary and middle school kids as a part of their school day. Since its inception, the School Program has taught over 400,000 kids to play chess.

Here are some of the benefits of chess as written by Christine Palm in her New York City Schools Chess Program Report in 1990:

- Chess instills in young players a sense of self-confidence and self-worth;
- Chess dramatically improves a child's ability to think rationally,
- Chess increases cognitive skills;
- Chess improves children's communication skills and aptitude in recognizing patterns;
- Chess results in higher grades, especially in English and Math studies,
- Chess builds a sense of team spirit while emphasizing the ability of the individual;
- Chess teaches the value of hard work, concentration and commitment;
- Chess makes a child realize that he or she is responsible for his or her own actions and must accept their consequences,
- Chess teaches children to try their best to win, while accepting defeat with grace;
- Chess provides an intellectual, comparative forum through which children can assert hostility i.e. "let off steam" in an acceptable way;
- Chess can become a child's most eagerly awaited school activity, dramatically improving attendance;

- Chess allows girls to compete with boys on a non-threatening, socially acceptable plane;
- Chess helps children make friends more easily because it provides an easy, safe forum for gathering and discussion,
- Chess allows students and teachers to view each other in a more sympathetic way,
- Chess, through competition, gives kids a palpable sign of their accomplishments, and finally;
- Chess provides children with a concrete, inexpensive and compelling way to rise above the deprivation and self-doubt which are so much a part of their lives.

Is chess for boys and girls?

In a word, yes. This is a question I wish we had grown past. The chess world, particularly the United States Chess Federation (USCF – which is discussed in Chapter 1), is working extremely hard to encourage girls to play chess. Although most scholastic tournaments are coed, there are tournaments specifically for girls only.

A word on pronouns in this book. I'm sensitive to the fact that some of you will be teaching your daughter, and some of you, your son. I have a daughter and two granddaughters, so I understand how it can feel when a book is written all about "he" and "him." I chose to roughly alternate between pronouns, so sometimes I'll be calling your child or your player a he and sometimes a her, as well as referring to your daughter or son. If this proves to be awkward, I apologize and hope you'll just mentally replace the pronouns as needed.

Teaching chess – some techniques

While playing chess is fun, teaching chess is flat out a blast. Teaching chess is really no different from teaching any other kind of board game, like Chutes and Ladders, Monopoly, or Risk. We start with the board [a map of the world – 64 light and dark squares] and the pieces [a colorful plastic marker – Knights and Rooks and Queens, oh my]. Then how to move, [roll the dice –

move the chess piece], the consequences of some moves [landing on Boardwalk with a hotel – putting your Knight where your opponent can take it for nothing] and how you win the game [take over the world in Risk – checkmate the King].

I'll grant you that chess is more complicated than those games and it will take longer than a few minutes for anyone, not just a child, to learn to play a complete game. However, it's still just teaching a game, and we break it down into small, easily digestible bits of information. Let me illustrate: The first time I took my then four-year-old son outside to play catch with his brand new glove, he did really well for the first three throws, then to my horror on the next one, he just didn't get the glove up high enough and the baseball sailed right over the web and smacked him in the forehead. Square on. We were only about six feet apart, so it mostly just made his eyes water and left a swell-looking red spot on which I'm pretty sure you could see a seam mark. After a little bit, we started up again and I took the "teaching moment" to tell him, again, to watch the ball go into the glove. What I didn't do is explain trajectory, ball speed, and anticipating the landing point because he wasn't ready for that advanced information. We'll keep things simple, until they aren't anymore, then we'll slow down even more to ensure both you and your child are first still having fun, and secondly that he's grasping the new concepts.

Chess is full of teaching moments, and nothing is quite as wonderful as when your child has an "ah ha" experience. It might be when she first sees a checkmate three moves ahead, or she might make a move you didn't expect, *and* it's a sound and strong move.

No one knows your son like you do. You know his personality, his likes, his dislikes. You know his limits. But one thing I've discovered over the years of coaching chess, is that young players will continually surprise you with their perceptiveness and understanding of the game far beyond your expectations. Don't sell your son short. Using patience and patience and patience, repeat the lesson until you're sure he's ready to move on. Sometimes you'll decide to move on and discover you need to backtrack a bit. Just remind your child of the forgotten information, and move ahead.

As you are playing a game with your son, keep in mind that mistakes will happen. He'll make a weak, maybe disastrous (from the game point of view) move, and the game would be over in just a few more moves. This is a teaching moment. One of my favorite and effective methods is the "Take-back" rule. It's just like it sounds. I tell my student to take back the move he just made, and look for a stronger one. I also immediately explain why the move was weak.

We all have our preferences in the way we communicate, and my choice is to label the move as "weak," rather than "bad." I know it's semantics, but as parent-teachers we must be careful not to let our daughter associate our criticism of a move with herself.

Rules – Just-in-time

The book of chess rules, *U.S. Chess Federation's Official Rules of Chess*, is 370 pages long. It covers so many topics, some of an obscure nature, that it can make a grownup cry. Don't ask your child to read it. *You* can read it if you want, and if your child is going to play competitively, you should. The rules that may seem obscure, in a tournament setting can make the difference between a win and a tie (a draw) or a win and a loss, or getting that draw instead of a loss. I will mention the rules that you *need* to know, when you (and your son) need to know them, so they'll be just-in-time.

Chapter 8 – A short rules list for tournament players covers the most common rules and problems a player will run into. Coaches: I recommend that you make copies of that chapter and give it to your players, covering it in detail in class.

Part One – Teaching Chess

Lesson 1 – The Board

Buying boards and sets.

Any board and chess set will do. Chess boards come in infinite colors, composition, and size, but one thing remains constant, the layout. Light squares and dark squares, 64 of them, 32 of each color. But certain boards are better for your daughter to learn with, and for you to teach with. You might have a very beautiful, and likely expensive, showcase set in your house, or you might have a plastic set that sells for about three or four bucks, the kind with red and black squares like a checker board. I don't recommend using either kind. The kind I suggest is one that has the Algebraic notation on it (next page).

Here's an alternative for you: if you prefer to buy a set locally for a lower price, go ahead, but it probably won't have algebraic notation. What I suggest is using masking tape along the edges and letter and number the board like the one on the next page.

When it's time to talk about the notation and what it's for and how to use it, we'll come back to it. For now, you need to know where to order a board like this. It's up to you how much you want to spend, but I recommend starting with what's called a tournament board and set. The

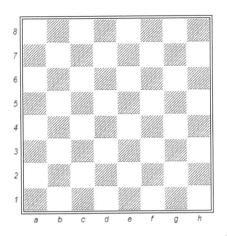

board is made of vinyl for easy transport to, yes you guessed it, tournaments, but actually anywhere. The pieces are large and durable. They pretty much bounce quite well off tile floors and come out unscathed. They also survive the washer and dryer. Don't ask. Where do I get these magical pieces? you ask. Well, it's up to you. One thing you can do is Google "Chess Sets" and start browsing the different online stores. Or you can go to www.uschess.org and shop there. This is the web site for the United States Chess Federation (USCF) and all of the items purchased through their store help support chess in the United States, including scholastic chess.

As soon as your set and board arrive, immediately use a permanent marker and put your daughter's initials on the felt bottom of *every* piece. Trust me on this. If you start going to clubs and / or tournaments, you'll see that many, many sets are identical. Then put her full name and school on the back of the vinyl board. Same reason.

Let's Play

When it's time for your son's first chess lesson, find a place where you and he can be comfortable. If he's on the young or small side, make sure the table you use is one where he can reach across it most of the way. There should be plenty of light. Chess players hate dim light. It's as though we're afraid we'll miss a brilliant move in the darkness. A bright overhead light is best.

Stash the board and set by the table, but not on it or in view. Keep the set in its carry bag (if you ordered one) or the bag it came in.

The board – explained

Get your child situated on his side of the table, then sit down across from him. For the first lesson, a little showmanship won't hurt. If you're using a rollup vinyl board, grab it by two corners, one in each hand, and unfurl it with a flick of the wrists. Let it settle onto the table like you're putting a tablecloth on. If you're using a solid board, deftly lift it to the table top and slide it into place. Arrange the board so row 1 is in front of your child. Invite him to touch it.

Let's introduce the board to your player. There are files a – h (go up and down) and ranks 1 – 8 (go left and right. I will generally call ranks rows because it's easier for kids – and me). We use the chess board's built-in grid along with a combination of a letter and number to identify each of the 64 squares. I call this the square's address, just as the house where you live has an address. When we say the square's address, it's always letter-number,

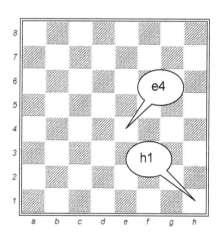

like e4 or h1 in the diagram. If your child has played the game Battleship, point out the similarities of calling out your hits or misses.

Now do this: poke a square and ask your son to say its name. Pick about ten or so at random. Then have your son touch the square and you call out its name. Mess up a couple of times and let him correct you. Look sheepish and say "oops" a lot. Trust me.

We're ready for light and dark. Simple I know, but poke a square and ask if it's light or dark. Do this to three or four squares. That's enough.

Rotate the board so row 1 is in front of you and row 8 is in front of your son. Repeat the little exercise of naming the squares. Players must become accustomed to seeing the board from both sides.

Lesson 2 – The Pieces

It's time for the really cool stuff. Pick up the bag, open it, and dump the pieces onto the board. Let them roll around. Let your son pick them up. If he's very young, five or so, don't be dismayed if he grabs the Knight and starts neighing. Ask him to put all the white pieces to the right (his) of the board. He may group them according to type, or he might just shove them around in no order. Either way is fine. You do the same with the black pieces.

White and Black. Oftentimes, you'll see sets where the pieces aren't actually white and black, but are, like one of my favorites, a rosewood for black and an oak-colored wood for white (on the cover). In any case, it'll always be a light color and a dark color, and we *always* call them White and Black.

Let's introduce the pieces' names and how many there are on each side. Hold up each piece and say its name. Invite your child to count how many he has. On the next page are the names of the pieces along with the symbol we'll use in this book, how many there are for each player, and the value for each piece.

The Pieces

Name	White symbol	Black symbol	Number for each player	Value
Pawn			8	1
Knight			2	3
Bishop			2	3
Rook			2	5
Queen			1	9
King			1	Not valued

There are a total of 16 pieces for each player.

You'll notice that the King is marked as "Not Valued" in the chart. The reason for this is that since the way to win the game is to checkmate the King, he can *never* be captured.

Spend a few minutes helping your child memorize the pieces' names and point values. Use pieces of both colors. Just hold up a piece and ask the name, and its value. Then, like you did with the squares, have your child hold up the piece and you say its name and value.

One method I use for helping a player understand the point value for the pieces is to equate them to dollars ($). If they know money, they'll understand piece values, believe me!

For a fun exercise, close this book and show your child the photo on the cover. Ask him to name all of the pieces in the photo. Then ask him to name the one piece that is missing. Answer: there is no Bishop.

Where do they all go?

This diagram shows where each piece goes on the board. In the next few steps, we'll place all of the pieces on the board, a few at a time. In diagrams, white is *always* shown at the bottom.

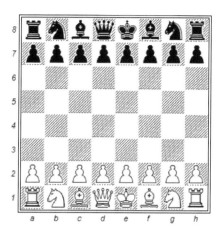

Setting up the board

1. Starting with the white pawns, have your child place all of them on row 2, one per square, while you put the black pawns on row 7.

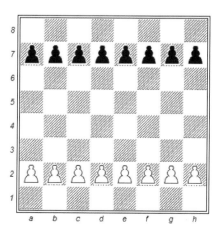

2. Put a Rook on each corner of row 1 and row 8; squares a1 and h1 for white, a8 and h8 for black.

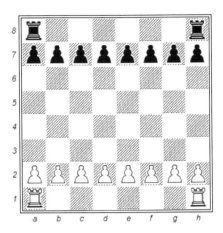

3. Place a Knight next to each Rook; squares b1 and g1 for white, b8 and g8 for black.

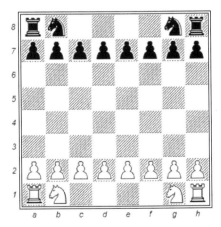

4. The Bishops go next to the Knights. Notice we're heading toward the middle of row 1 and row 8; c1 and f1 for white, c8 and f8 for black.

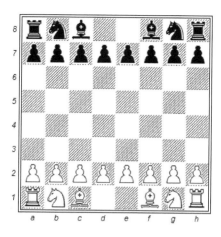

We have all the pieces on the board except the Queen and King. Before we go any farther, a couple of points to mention. Look at the board. The square on your child's right in row 1, and the square on your right in row 8, is white. If you ever play on a board without Algebraic notation imprinted on it, you must remember to set up the board with "white on the right." However, players using algebraic boards sometimes set them up sideways, or switch row one and eight so that the pieces start in incorrect positions. Teach your child to always double-check the board before setting up the pieces.

The pieces are currently perfectly symmetrical. Each of you has a Rook, Knight and Bishop on both your right and left sides. However, this changes with the placement of the Queen and King because the Queen always goes on her own color.

5. Have your child place the white Queen on the only uncovered white (light) square, d1 and you put the black Queen on the only uncovered black (dark) square, d8.

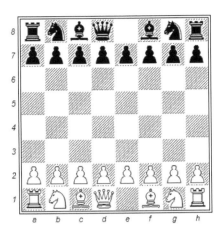

6. Now, both of you put your Kings on the only square left. Your child's King is on his right, your King is on your *left* and the Kings are on the same file, "e," while the Queens are opposite each other on file "d." Your board is now set up properly.

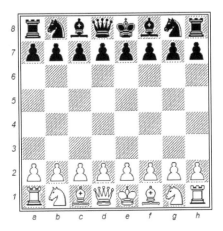

Lesson 3 – How the pieces move

Teacher alert: if you are already familiar with chess notation, please continue, but if you are not, please read Lesson 4 – Reading Chess Notation, for your benefit, then came back to this point. Later, when you reach Lesson 4 for your child, teach it to her then.

Before we talk about how each piece moves, here are a few words on capturing your opponent's pieces. It's not like checkers. You do not jump a piece to capture it. Instead, take your opponent's piece off the board and put yours on the now vacant square. In order for a piece to capture another, the attacking piece must have a legal move to the square occupied by your opponent's piece.

For all pieces except the King, there will be a game for you and your child to play. The purpose of the games is two-fold:

1. To get your child's hands on the pieces right away and sling them around the board, and
2. to start the process of embedding (or ingraining) each piece's move in your child's mind. This is similar to the process of learning to throw a baseball (softball). At first, it's obvious that a kid is thinking about how to throw: correct foot forward, arm back, weight shift, arm forward,

let go of the ball at the right point. In chess, new players do the same thing, thinking about how the piece moves, rather than what they want to accomplish with a move.

As with anything, practice improves play.

Pawn

Overview

- Moves straight ahead, except when capturing.
- If another piece (white or black) is on the square directly in front of the pawn, it is blocked and cannot move.
- Cannot move backwards.
- On the first move only, can move either one or two squares.
- Captures only on the diagonal.

The pawn's moves

On a pawn's first move (and only on the pawn's first move), the player has the choice of moving the pawn straight ahead one square:

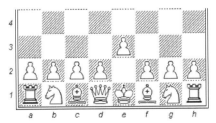

or two.

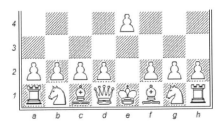

White could move the pawn resting on e2 to e3, or to e4, but only on the e2 pawn's first move. I know this is a little like saying you can do something if it's Tuesday and raining, but there it is. This rule of one-or-two led chess organizations to create a special move, *en passant*, which we'll discuss later.

After the first move, whether it was one or two squares, a pawn can only move one square at a time straight ahead. If something is in the road, another piece, either white or black, the pawn is blocked and cannot advance.

Here it's white's move. The e4 pawn is blocked by black's pawn on e5. However, the d4 pawn can move to d5. And here's another "however:" the d4 pawn can capture black's e5 pawn because pawns capture on the diagonal. A pawn attacks only two squares at any time, so white's d pawn attacks c5 and e5.

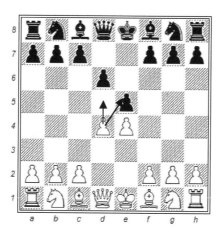

Point out that white can capture black (d4xe5, we read this as d4 "takes" e5) and that black can capture white (e5xd4)! It depends on whose move it is. When two opposing pieces can capture each other, but do not, this is called tension.

Capturing practice – pawn

Set up the board like this, then ask your child to make the only possible capture for white (exd5).

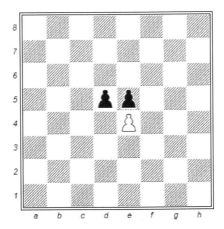

Set up the board like this, and ask your child to capture all of the black pawns. Your child will need to think about this one. For example: if the first capture is cxd4, and the rest of the captures go up and to the right (dxe5, exf5) we can't capture the c5 pawn. Our solution is: cxd5, dxc5, exf5, fxe5 – a crisscross pattern.

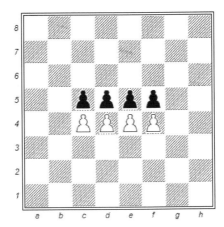

RONN MUNSTERMAN

Concept – protecting pieces

We need to teach your child the all-important concept of how to protect pieces, and the difference between a protected piece and a non-protected piece. We'll focus on the pawn because the upcoming game "The Pawn Game" will have only pawns on the board.

We saw on pages 21 and 22 how pawns capture, on the diagonal, and on the same color square as the one they were sitting on. Remind your player that the pawn *never* moves backward.

First the definitions:

1. protected piece – when one of your pieces attacks (can land on) a square where another of your pieces sits, the latter piece is protected.
2. unprotected piece – when a piece has no friendly pieces attacking the square it is sitting on.

To illustrate, let's look at pawns that are protected and some that are unprotected. In this diagram, we see white pawns on e4, and d3, and a black pawn on d5, and the rest for each side on row 2 or 7. It's black's move. Show your player that the e4 pawn sits on a square that the d3 pawn can attack. This means the e4 pawn is protected. If black captures e4, then white can capture back by moving dxe4.

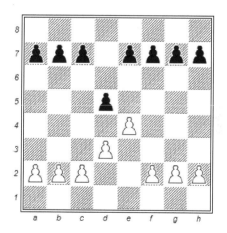

Point out that black's d5 pawn has no friendly pawns that can protect it. Since it's black's move, ask your child to find the two moves that can protect the d5 pawn. Answer: c6 and e6 (next two diagrams). This is important, make sure your child sees this clearly.

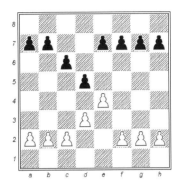 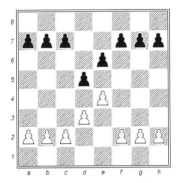

Set up the board as shown in this diagram. Name each of white's pawns and ask whether it is protected or unprotected. If your player gets them all right the first time, Excellent! If not, repeat a few times until he does.

Answers:
a – unprotected
b – protected by the a pawn
c – unprotected
d – protected by the c pawn
e – protected by the d *and* f pawn
f – unprotected
g – protected by the f pawn
h – unprotected

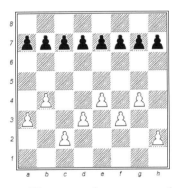

The previous diagram is meant to illustrate the protected – unprotected idea, and is not one that would be considered a strong pawn structure during a game.

Concept – passed pawn

A pawn that has no opposing pawns on the file to either side and toward the pawn's front, and no opposing pawn in front of it, is a passed pawn. This is because now, only larger, more valuable pieces can stop the pawn from reaching the 8th rank (See Pawn Promotion next). In this diagram, the white pawn on e5 is a passed pawn, even though the black pawn on d5 is on the file next to it, the d5 pawn cannot capture the e5 pawn. Black's d5 pawn is not a passed pawn because it has a pawn in front of it on d2 and a pawn to one side and in front on c2. This knowledge will be important in the upcoming Pawn Game.

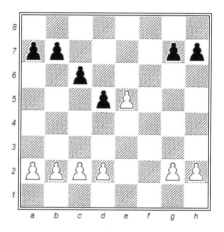

Pawn Promotion

Any pawn that reaches its own 8th rank, that is, the rank at the far side of the board, can be promoted to any piece except the King. Almost all players promote the pawn to a Queen, and many scholastic sets now come with an extra Queen for each side. It is therefore possible to have nine Queens. However, I always caution my players not to have more than two Queens (assuming the opponent has one or less). This is due to the fact that the likelihood of stalemate increases as does the number of Queens.

Briefly, stalemate is when the opposing King is NOT in check AND cannot move to a square without moving into check, AND no other friendly piece can move (such as a pawn that is blocked from moving). This results in a tie and both players get ½ point. This is not very satisfying for the player with the Queen advantage who should have earned a whole point, but got a half-point, and exciting for the opposing player who should have gotten a zero, but got a half-point instead.

If extra Queens are unavailable, players typically use an upside down Rook to represent the Queen. There's more on Queening the Pawn in Lesson 11.

Ask your player if he has any questions about pawn captures. If he has some, answer them and / or go back through the past few pages. Once those questions are answered, or if he has no questions, ask him if he's ready to play the Pawn Game. Act excited!

The Pawn Game

Rather than go through all of the pieces and their moves at one time, we're going to learn about each piece, then play a game that illustrates that piece's move, and give your child some practice, starting with the Pawn Game.

With your child playing white, set up all the pawns (8 of each color), her white ones on row 2 and your black ones on row 7.

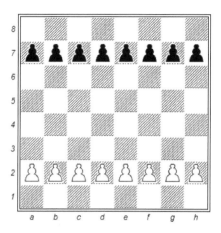

Rules:
1. White moves first.
2. I highly recommend that you get your daughter to move the d and e pawns first. This will help get her into the practice of doing that. This will be important later when we start talking about the opening moves of a game.
3. First player to get a pawn to the 8th rank wins. This means white must move a pawn all the way across the board to row 8, while you must try to get a pawn to row 1.
4. Alternate colors after each game. Play about three games.

Pawn Special Move – *en passant*

This rule causes more confusion and uncertainty than any other. Some coaches prefer to wait to teach this rule, and I am one of them, however, I'm including it here so you can easily find it later. A good time to teach this is after you've played a few complete games.

En passant is French for "in passing" and is directly related to a player's choice of moving a pawn one or two squares on the first move. Here, white has moved his e pawn to e5 (made up of the moves 1. e4 and 2. e5) while black has moved c5. It is black's move. If he wants to move his d pawn, he can choose to move it to either d6 or d5.

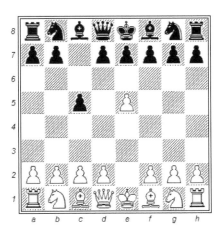

If he moves to d6, white can (if he chooses) capture the pawn by moving 3. exd6. If black moves 2. . . . d5, he has "passed" white's e pawn on e5 like cars on a two lane highway.

In this case, white can use *en passant* (there's no need for the player to say it out loud) and capture the pawn on d5 by placing his own pawn, not on d5, but on d6, *as if the pawn has moved to d6.* So in either case, the diagram shows the result, and the move is recorded as 3. exd6.

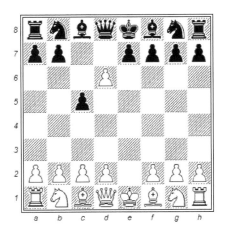

RONN MUNSTERMAN

Rook

Overview

- Moves up and down (along the files) or side-to-side (on the rows).
- Can capture any opposing piece along its path, but can be blocked by a piece of its own color (friendly).
- Can touch every square on the board.
- Very powerful, especially if two are working together as a team on the same file or row (often called a battery, an old artillery term).

Here we see the full range of a Rook. Remember, if a friendly piece is on a square along its path, the Rook is blocked. If it's an opposing piece, the Rook can capture it.

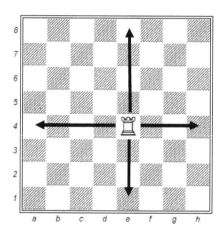

Pawn and Rook game

Rules
1. Set up the board with all the pawns as in the Pawn game.
2. Put the Rooks in the corners on row 1 and 8.
3. Remove the four d and e pawns. This gives the Rooks some running room right away.
4. White moves first.
5. The first player to capture all six of the opponent's pawns, or gets a pawn to the 8th rank wins.

Important note: remind your child about pawns that protect each other. You don't want to capture a pawn protected by another pawn with a Rook because this is a poor exchange for the player with the Rook (5 points given up for 1 point).

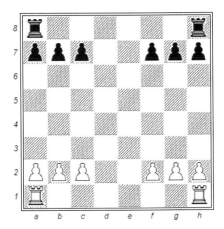

Bishop

Overview

- Moves diagonally.
- There is a light and a dark Bishop, meaning the color of the square they started from.
- Can only land on squares that match the color of the square where it started.
- Can capture any opposing piece along its path, but can be blocked by a piece of its own color (friendly).

There are never two Bishops on the same square color for the same player (ignoring the possible event that a pawn is promoted to a Bishop).

The Bishop's moves
White's light-squared Bishop

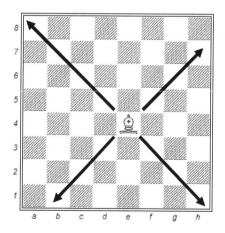

White's dark-squared Bishop

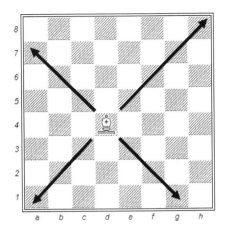

Pawn and Bishop game

Rules
1. Set up the board with all the pawns as in the Pawn game.
2. Put the white Bishops on c1 and f1, the black Bishops on c8 and f8.
3. Remove the four d and e pawns. This gives the Bishops an opening at the start.
4. White moves first.
5. The first player to capture all six of the opponent's pawns, or gets a pawn to the 8th rank, wins.

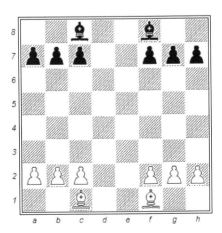

Queen

Overview

1. Moves in any direction.
2. The Queen's move is a combination of a Rook and Bishop.
3. Can capture any opposing piece along its path, but can be blocked by a piece of her own color (friendly).
4. She's the most powerful piece on the board and you have to treat her with respect and make sure to be careful where you place her, because your opponent would love to capture your Queen with a lower-valued piece.

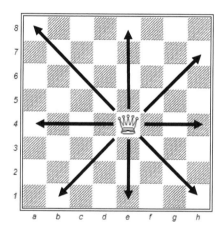

Queen and Pawn game – Queen Running Amuck

Rules
1. Set up the board with all the black pawns as in the Pawn game, however,
2. Place a white Queen on d1 (no pawns for white!)
3. The player with the Queen tries to capture all of the opposing pawns.
4. White moves first.
5. If the player with Queen captures all the pawns, then he wins, however, if one pawn makes it to the 8th rank, that player wins.
6. Reverse sides and play a few more games.

King

Overview

- He is the most important piece on the board, but not the most powerful.
- Moves one square at a time, is as slow as a pawn.
- Moves in any direction.
- Remember, the only way to win is to checkmate the opponent's King, so our responsibility is to keep our own King safe and sound.

The King's moves

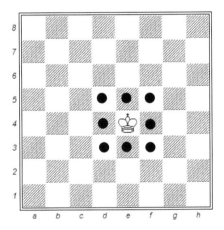

Knight

Overview

I always save the Knight for last because he has the most complicated move, however, do not tell your child this. She'll discover this on her own. If you tell her, she might become apprehensive and may not use the Knight correctly, or at all. I've known chess players who exchanged their Knights to get them off the board because they don't feel comfortable playing with them. Don't allow this from your child. All pieces have a part to play in the game.

- The Knights are the King's horsemen, just like the Knights of old. Like the horse they represent, they can jump over pieces! The Knight is the only piece that is not blocked by another piece.
- The move is an L-shaped "one up and two over" or "two up and one over" pattern. The up can be replaced with "down."
- Depending on where the Knight is on the board, he can attack up to eight squares at the same time.
- The Knight always lands on a square whose color is different from the one where he currently sits.

The Knight's moves

Dark to light colored square

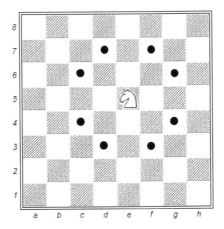

Light to dark colored square

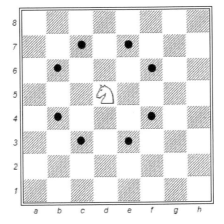

RONN MUNSTERMAN

Knights are at their most powerful toward the center of the board. Many new players put the knight on or near the edge of the board. Discourage this. Here's why:

Example of Knights on or near the edge of the board. White's Knight loses two attack squares (one-fourth), and black's Knight loses four, (one-half) of his attack squares!

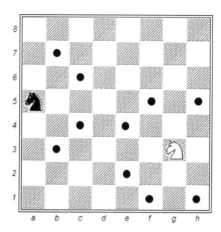

Time for the horse races!

Rules:

1. The white player puts a Knight on g1 and the black player puts one on b8.
2. Taking turns, each player moves his Knight toward the opponent's back rank.
3. The first one to get there wins that race.
4. Have three or four races and add a second Knight for each player. Then, the first one to get both Knights to the opponent's back row wins.

Review time

You've both been working for a while now and it may be a good time for a break. Go do that, then come back for review.

1. Clear all the pieces off the board.
2. Call out a square's address and have your child point to it. Do as many as you think are necessary.
3. Hold up a piece and ask your child its name and point value. Do at least one of each kind, and mix in black and white pieces.
4. Have your child set up the white pieces. Be sure to check the positions, especially of the Queen and King – remember, "Queen on her own color."
5. Rotate the board so the black side is in front of your child. Have him set up the black pieces. Again, check the positions, especially of the Queen and King, which will be reversed from his point of view as related to the way white is set up.
6. Clear all the pieces from the board.
7. Put each piece, one at a time, from the pawn to the King, on the board and have your child show you how it moves.

Repeat this review until you're confident your child has it all. Always be aware that you may need to remind your player of something, often the same thing – patience, please.

♟ ♜ ♞ ♝ ♛ ♚

Lesson 4 – Reading Chess Notation

It's time to discuss chess notation in detail. From this lesson forward, all moves will be described using chess notation. Instead of saying the white Queen captured black's pawn on g7, we say, or write:

6. Qxg7 . . .

Here's what each part of this notation means:

"6." – the move number
"Q" – the symbol for the Queen
"x" – stands for "takes" or "captures"
"g7" – the square the Queen moved to
" . . . " – indicates black's move is next. If it's expressed like this: 6. . . . Nf5, it means white has already moved, but isn't shown.

So it's read like this: Move 6, Queen takes g7. Note that we don't write the letter for the piece that was taken. We write where the moving piece landed. Here are the symbols for all of the pieces, except the pawn, which we'll come back to:

K – King
Q – Queen
R – Rook
B – Bishop
N – Knight (notice we can't use K because that belongs to the King)

Pawns are identified by the file they sit on. At the beginning of the game there are pawns on each file, so there's an "a," "b," "c," "d," "e," "f," "g," and "h" pawn for both colors. During a game, since pawns capture on the diagonal, they often change from one file to one of the two next to the one they're sitting on. When we write the move for a pawn, we identify only the file, not the file and row. For example, here it's white's move.

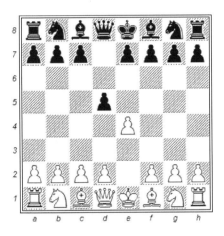

When we play:
2. exd5 . . .
we have two d pawns for white (one on d2 and one on d5). How do we know which one is which when we want to move one and record the move? If we move d2 to d4, we write:
3. d4 . . .
If we moved the pawn on d5 to d6:
3. d6.

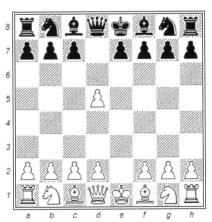

Since we know a pawn can't move backwards, we can always tell which pawn was moved by where it ended up, as only one pawn can go there.

Here is a list of all of the symbols used in chess notation.

Piece	Symbol
King	K
Queen	Q
Rook	R
Bishop	B
Knight	N
pawn	file letter

Action	Symbol
Capture	x
Check	+
Checkmate	# or ++
Castle-Kingside	O-O
Castle-Queenside	O-O-O
Pawn promotion	=

Comments on a move

! a particularly good (and usually surprising) move
!! an excellent move
? a bad move
?? a blunder
!? an interesting move that may not be best
?! a dubious move - one which may turn out to be bad

Lesson 5 – Checkmate patterns

We're almost ready for a game. This lesson introduces the point of the game, or how to win: checkmate. You will teach your child what checkmate is using examples of it that are called checkmate patterns. It is crucial that your child grasps these concepts and learns to recognize a checkmate pattern. One of the byproducts of this particular lesson is that while your child is learning how to checkmate a King, she will also be learning one of the most important ideas in chess: the combination. If you've watched *Searching for Bobby Fischer*, which I mentioned in the Introduction, you might recall the scene where Laurence Fishburn's character is yelling at Mrs. Waitzkin as she's dragging little Josh away from the players in the park. "Lady, your son is using combinations! He attacks with combinations!" She has no idea what that means, but chess players watching the movie know. And your child is about to know this fundamentally important skill. With very few exceptions (later, we'll take a look at one: the Back row Mate), a King cannot be checkmated by one piece alone. Please remember this because that's why the combination is so important to be able to achieve checkmate.

How to use this lesson

Each checkmate pattern has two diagrams, the first one is before the move that calls checkmate, the second one is after the move for checkmate. Set up the board as shown in the first diagram. First ask your player if he "sees" the checkmate move. If he does, have him make the move he sees. If he has picked a move that is not checkmate (show him why it is not) or he doesn't see one, show him the move as shown in the second diagram. Work through all of the patterns in the same manner. At the end of the examples, we'll move into a review and I'll make some suggestions on how to reinforce the patterns in your child's memory.

Checkmate and checkmate patterns

Checkmate defined:
1. When you attack the King with one (or more) of your pieces,
2. AND the King cannot move away from the attack,
3. AND a defending piece cannot block the attack,
4. AND the attacking piece cannot be captured.

A word on the checkmate pattern diagrams: these illustrate the actual checkmate, but there would be other pieces on the board that are not shown. The assumption is that black has no piece that can save the King by capturing the checkmating piece, or of blocking it. The checkmate patterns are based on the idea of "mate-in-one" and in each one, it's white's move.

So what does checkmate look like? It has many faces, but a checkmate combination (pieces working together) typically must have two pieces attacking the same square. This is an important thing to point out to your child: the checkmate square is often the one square where both of white's pieces can move to. However, only one of them can create the checkmate, the other protects the checkmating piece. Notice I said "typically." That's because some checkmates can be created by pieces that are not next to the opponent's King. See Patterns 4 and 6.

Checkmate Pattern 1 – Queen and Knight

In this example, the Queen and Knight both attack g7, the checkmate square.

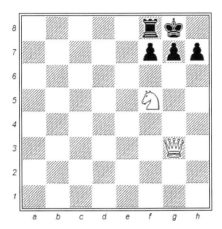

Here, the white Queen has just captured black's pawn on g7, checkmate! In chess notation this move is: Qxg7#. The pound sign indicates checkmate. A single plus sign (+) indicates check. When writing on paper, some players use the pound sign (#) and others use two plus signs (++) for checkmate. Either is okay.

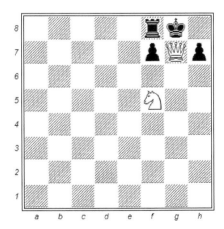

How do we know this is checkmate?

1. First we determine whether black can capture the attacking Queen. The King can't do that because the Knight on f5 is supporting (protecting) the Queen (because the Knight can also move to g7). This is a combination of the Queen and Knight. The black Rook can't capture the Queen because she's on a square the Rook cannot legally move to.

2. Then we look for pieces that can block the Queen's attack. There are none because she is on the square right next to the King.

3. The last hope is to examine squares the King *could* move to. In this case, it would be only h8 because all other squares are occupied. He cannot legally move there because the Queen is also attacking *that* square.

4. Therefore: checkmate!

Close this book and show your child the photo on the cover. It is this checkmate pattern!

Checkmate Pattern 2 – Queen and Knight

The Queen and Knight are both attacking h7.

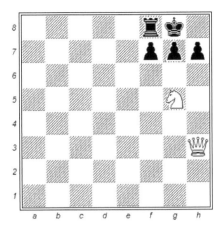

When the Queen captures h7, it's checkmate. Qxh7#.

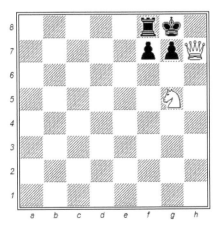

RONN MUNSTERMAN

Checkmate Pattern 3 – Queen and Rook

The Queen and Rook are attacking h7.

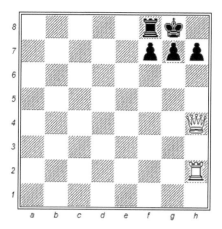

The move is Qxh7#.

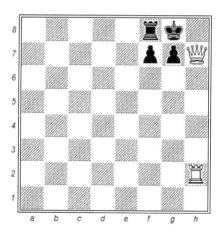

Checkmate Pattern 4 – Bishop and Rook

This checkmate is different from the first three where the Queen prevented the King from escaping because she attacked his escape squares.

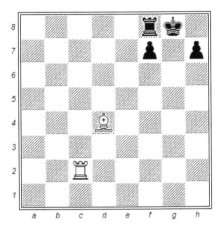

In this case, the Rook calls check by moving to g2 (Rg2#). The Bishop prevents the King from escaping to h8.

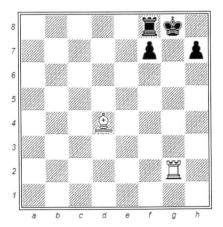

RONN MUNSTERMAN

Checkmate Pattern 5 – Queen and Bishop

The Queen and Bishop are attacking g7.

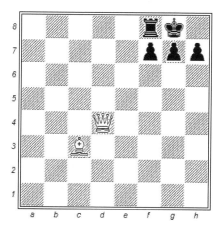

The Queen captures g7 for checkmate (Qxg7#).

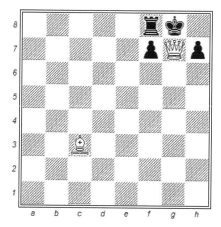

Checkmate Pattern 6 – Two Rooks

The Rook on the h file is the key to this pattern – he prevents the King's escape.

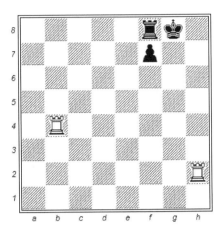

Rook moves to g4, checkmate (Rg4#).

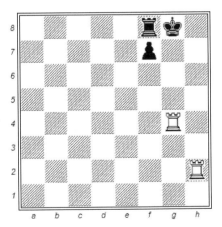

RONN MUNSTERMAN

Checkmate Pattern 7 – Back row Mate, Rook or Queen

New players are especially susceptible to this checkmate. It occurs when the back row is unguarded and the King, although apparently safe behind his pawns after castling, faces an opposing Rook or Queen on the loose, which can end the game abruptly. Here's what it may look like. The Rook on e3 has an opening to black's back row.

By moving Re8#, white gets a surprise checkmate. There are no black pieces on the back row to help out. The only way for black to avoid this is if he has a piece that can be moved to the back row in time, or if he can move one of the pawns to give himself an escape square, before the checkmate move of course!

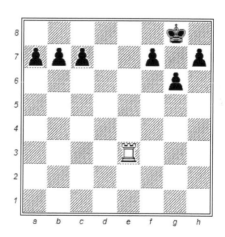

Review checkmate patterns

You've taken your child through the basic patterns. It's time to review. Three good ways to do this are:

1. Go though the patterns again, but in a different order than presented the first time.

2. Reverse colors. Rotate the board and have your child make the move for black instead of white. Here's one example:

3. You can set up the board more like what would be found in a game and have your child make the checkmate move for white. Here's an example, where the Queen checkmates the King by capturing

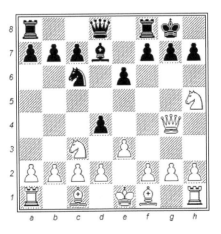

the pawn on g7 as shown in the very first checkmate pattern. Note that the Knight is on h5 instead of f5.

Lesson 6 – Playing the game

There are many checkmate patterns, but we've covered a few of the most common. Now, let's move on to playing a game. One of the things that often happens with young, new players, is they don't know quite what to do, so they copy, or mirror your moves. Don't let your child do this. For that reason, we're going to first talk about parts of the game, then illustrate moves, using a complete (but relatively short) game.

Parts of the Game

A chess game is divided into three parts:
1. Opening
2. Middle
3. End

Each part of the game has its own definition and as we go through the next few lessons, you'll be teaching your player what those definitions are. Remind your player that since we are always looking for checkmate opportunities, checkmate can occur in any of the parts of the game.

Opening

The opening is generally defined as "about" the first eight to ten moves. This is not a rule. We don't count our moves and when we reach eight say to ourselves, "Oh, the opening is over, now for the middle game." No, this is merely a guideline. What matters more is that the opening's three goals are met:
1. control the center
2. develop pieces
3. protect the King

Control the center

If we think of the center of the board as being like a bottleneck on a heavily traveled road, we can visualize that to get to our opponent's King, we have to squeeze through the narrow opening. The exact center of the board is made up of the four squares d4, d5, e4 and e5 (the small box). The expanded center contains sixteen squares as shown in the larger box.

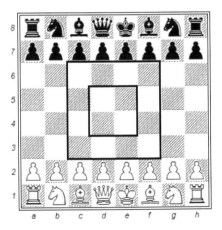

Controlling the center in our opening moves means to *occupy* or *attack* as many of these center squares as possible. Here's another way to look at controlling the center in terms of sports:

- Baseball – a catcher protecting the plate or the runner slides around him to score.
- Football – the line of scrimmage, the offense opens a hole for the runner or the defense plugs it up.
- Basketball – the lane (in the paint), keeping the offensive player from the basket or weaving through the defense to score.

Develop minor pieces

Developing our minor pieces (Knights and Bishops) means to get our material (introducing another word for pieces) into a position where they help *control* the center as soon as possible. The sooner we get our pieces out there into play, the more likely it is we might be able to achieve a slight advantage over our opponent. And believe me, sometimes it is this small advantage that gets us the win.

I call the idea of developing the minor pieces as getting your pieces over (or outside) the fence, the fence being the pawn line, and this helps new players understand it.

Protect the King

There's a special move in chess, involving the King and a Rook, called castling. This castling move allows the King to move two squares at one time and the involved Rook either two or three squares. In chess terminology, when the castling Rook moves two squares, we are castling the short side, and when it moves three, the long side.

When you can castle:
- The King has not moved AND the Rook involved has not moved.
- The squares between the King and Rook are empty.
- The King is not in check.
- A square the King must cross is not under attack by an opposing piece. The Rook may cross over an attacked square.

Although the rules don't require it, it's been my experience in the scholastic world that it's better to teach young players to move the King first, because that is a clear indicator to the opponent that castling is taking place. The point of this is that some believe, incorrectly, that if you touch the Rook first, it's not castling, and try to force the player to move the Rook only. As I just said, although the rules don't require the King to be moved first, a young player whose misinformed opponent yells out, "You touched your Rook, you can't castle!" can become overly upset to the point he can't concentrate and ends up losing the game.

Let's illustrate castling by examining the diagrams on the next two pages. To castle for white, move the King to g1, then in the same move, put the Rook on f1. For black, the King goes on g8 and the Rook on f8. I like to refer to the Rook's move as hopping over the King. The kids like it. Castling can be done either to the King's right or his left. Again, the "type" of castling is determined by how many spaces are in-between the King and the Rook: short (King side) is when there are two spaces, and long (Queen side) is when there are three spaces.

Short (King) side

Before castling

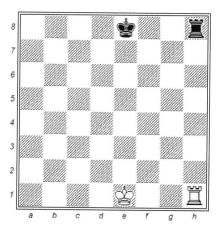

After castling

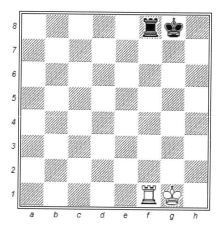

Long (Queen) side

Before castling

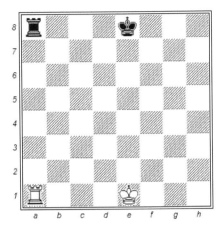

After castling

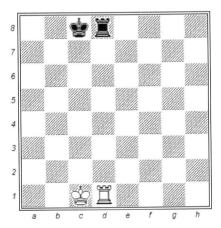

Here's an example of not being able to castle. The black Bishop is attacking f1. Since the King must cross f1 to get to g1, castling is not allowed.

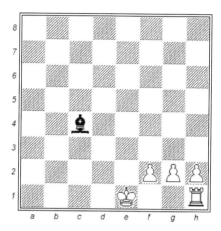

Here's an example of castling when the Rook crosses a square under attack (b1), which is okay. The King moves to c1 and the Rook crosses the attack to d1.

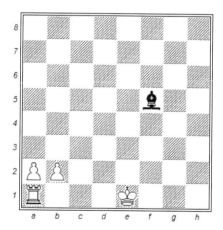

In chess notation the castling move is written as "O-O" when the King moves to the short side, and is written "O-O-O" when castling to the long side.

Back to the board

We're ready to see an opening in action. Set up the board, again having your child play white. Remind your child that white *always* moves first and have him start the game. We're going to start with the Ruy Lopez opening. This is a solid opening for white with a long history. The Ruy Lopez is named after a 16th century Spanish chess player and priest, Ruy Lopez de Segura. The first known book published on chess, the *Göttingen Manuscript* – 1490, included the opening, although the opening only gained Lopez's name after he wrote a book on it in 1561.

If you're familiar with the Ruy Lopez, you'll notice this is slightly different from "book." This is so the first opening illustrates our points and each player has a solid foundation, or starting point to play from. (Book means the expected move sequence.)

Here we go. Both you and your child make the moves below as you read them out loud.

1. e4	e5
2. Nf3	Nc6
3. Bb5	d6
4. Nc3	Bd7
5. d3	Nf6
6. Bg5	Be7
7. 0-0	0-0

Now let's check our board. If yours looks exactly like this, excellent work. If not, reset the board to its starting point and try again.

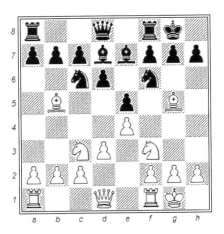

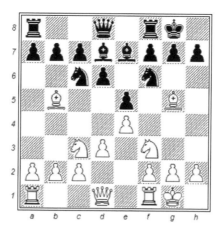

Referring to the diagram above, let's see how we did on our opening goals:

Controlling the center

- White and black both have four pieces in the expanded center of the board (two pawns and two Knights). Ask your child to point them out to you.
- The white Bishops are on black's half of the board.
- Black's two Bishops are not in the expanded center, but they attack, or in this case, guard the Knights that are in the center.

Developing the minor pieces

- All of the minors pieces (Knights and Bishops) have moved and are in the middle of the action.
- A note here about developing the minor pieces: generally, it's not considered good practice to move the same piece twice in the opening, however, as with most things there can be exceptions, such as seeing an opportunity to capture a piece or the piece in question is under attack and unprotected, but in the early stages of your child's

chess career, let's get him to focus on moving all of the minor pieces once, before moving one for a second time.

Protecting the King

- Castling complete.

Review

1. Have your child name the three parts of the game:
   a. Opening
   b. Middle game
   c. End game
2. Name the minor pieces:
   a. Knights
   b. Bishops
3. Name the three goals of the opening:
   a. Controlling the center – occupy or attack a center square.
   b. Developing the minor pieces.
   c. Protecting the King – castling.
4. Reset the board and replay the opening two or three more times, alternating colors.

Note on colors

I highly recommend that you have your player alternate playing white and black. New players are often "given" white in deference to their newness to the game, but this can create a near phobia of playing with the black pieces. Encourage your player to play both colors, and it's wise not to make a big deal out of white's "advantage" of always moving first. Among new players, this advantage is negligible.

Lesson 7 – Middle game & Chess weapons

Okay, so now what? One of the problems chess players, even experienced ones, run into after the opening is exactly this question. The opening moves often take only a minute or two, when both players know the opening and its variations. If you're watching a game, it seems like a flurry of activity and suddenly one player stops and her clock just seems to be ticking away. This is because she is weighing the possibilities. Every position has many, many possibilities, and to examine them all might not be realistic, but to examine the most common and effective ones goes faster. We'll talk about this "thought process" in Lesson 12 – Thinking, Chess Calculations.

There are two goals in the middle game:

1. checkmate your opponent – this is *always* the first thing we look for.
2. gain an advantage in material – capturing more value of pieces than your opponent.

There's another goal, gaining space, but that's not in the scope of this book. Briefly, it means to control more of the board than your opponent and restrict his options for movement.

For our purposes, we'll stick to the two goals. Here's the really cool stuff: Chess Weapons. A word on a word: weapon – if using this word just doesn't sit well with you, I'm not going to try and convince you, except to say that chess is a battle, and all battles use weapons of some sort, whether it's a sword or our intellect, a weapon is in use. However, for your comfort, you can substitute "tactics" for weapons.

For this lesson, clear off the board and set up the pieces as shown in the diagrams. Show your child the move that creates the attack. Let him examine the result on the board. Move the attacked piece and ask him what would happen. This will help him see the whole picture.

Weapons – Pins and Forks and Skewers, Oh my!

Pin

A pin sticks a defending piece against another defending piece of *higher* value. Here we have a pin that occurs frequently. The white Bishop on b5 is attacking the black Knight on c6. You may recall this from the Ruy Lopez opening we saw in Lesson 6. The problem for black is that the King on e8 is on the same diagonal as the Knight and white's Bishop. If black moves the Knight, the King is in check from the white Bishop, which is an illegal move. This is the pin.

In the next diagram, black has created the pin

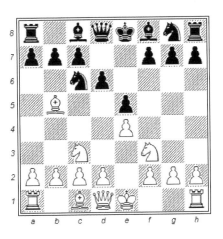

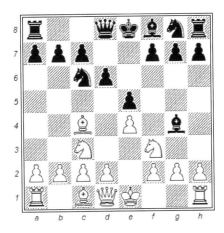

on the Knight on f3. If white moves the Knight, the black Bishop, can capture the Queen. A Bishop for a Queen! Players live for this exchange. Remember, the Bishop is valued at three points and the Queen at nine.

So how do we defend a pin? One way is to place another, lower valued piece between the pinned piece (Knight) and the higher valued piece (Queen). Here, white moves the light Bishop backwards to e2. This means that any time white wants to move the Knight, he can, and his Bishop will be attacking the black Bishop and be supported by the Queen.

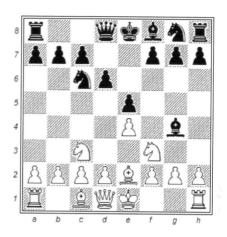

Fork

A fork occurs when a piece attacks two or more of the opponent's pieces at the same time and generally speaking, both are of higher value than the attacker. The Knight fork is the most common, so let's look at it first. With the move 5. Nxf7, the Knight captures the f7 pawn and attacks the Rook on h8 and the Queen *at the same time*. Since the Knight is protected by the Bishop on c4, there is nothing for black to do here except move the Queen to d7 or e7. White captures the

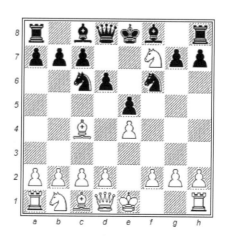

Rook, giving up a 3-point piece for a 5-pointer. Plus, if black mishandles it, white could get the Rook and the Knight escapes completely.

There are endless possibilities for Knight forks and they're quite effective because, typically, the defender never sees it coming. Here's another with hapless Rooks as victims. Nc2!

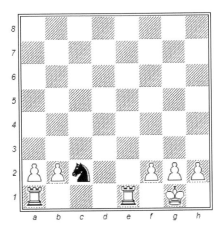

Followed by the best of them all, the royal fork, where the Knight attacks the Queen and Rook while calling check. Not a fun place to be if you're playing white. Nf3+.

Here's a Bishop fork that wins the game for white. White sees that black's King and Rook are on the same diagonal. The move is Be5+. The King is forced to move and the Rook is captured. Then all white has to do is march the "a" pawn in for a Queen. See Lesson 11 – End Game, Rule of the square.

One more fork, but with a lowly pawn. The "e" pawn is shoved up one square and forks the Bishop and Knight. The important thing here is that the pawn is guarded by the Rook (otherwise the Bishop would just snap up the pawn). It would work also, if the f pawn was sitting on f4.

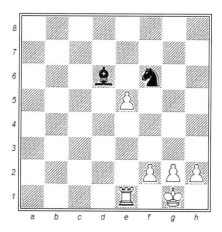

Skewer

The skewer is a reverse pin where the higher valued piece is between the attacker and another friendly piece. Here, the King is skewered against the Queen when the Rook calls check by Rc8+. When the King moves out of check, the Rook runs down the row and snags the Queen.

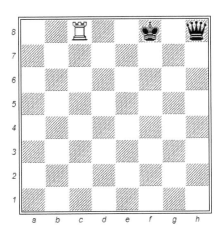

Discovered attack with check. Ouch!

One of the most devastating moves is to call check by moving a piece out of the way, and typically the moving piece attacks another piece while the piece behind calls check. In this position, the Rook is lurking behind the Bishop. The move is Be7+ (diagram next page, or Bd2+, not shown). The Bishop moves, attacking the Queen from e7 while the Rook, newly discovered, calls check on the King without even moving. Check always take priority, so the King must move and the Queen falls. By the way, black could move Qg4 to block the check, but will still lose the Queen with Rxg4+.

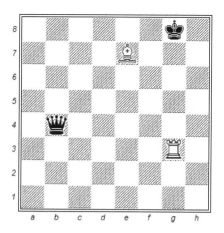

Oops – the Hanging piece

A piece that is unprotected *and* under attack by an opposing piece is said to be a "hanging piece" because it's just hanging there, all by its lonesome. New players "hang" pieces all the time, so don't be dismayed when your child hangs something, and often more than once per game. Trust me. This is a good time to use a "take-back move," which I talk about in Lesson 14.

First, let's show your player what a hanging piece looks like. Set up your board like the diagram below.

It's black's move. Do you see the hanging white piece? The Knight moved to g5 and is sitting there by himself with no protection while being attacked by black's Queen. Ask your player to find and capture the hanging piece.

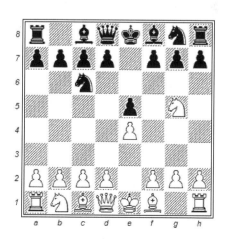

Let's find the hanging piece in this more complicated position.

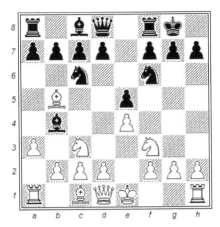

This position occurred after 5. . . . . O-O. Do you see the problem for black? He overlooked the attack on his Bishop on b4, and castled instead of moving the Bishop to safety. White plays 6. axb4, winning the Bishop outright.

Exchanges –Up, Down, or Even?

Exchanges, the capture and capture-back sequence (or multiple captures), can be defined as one of the following: up, down or even. The terms simply mean that from one player's perspective, he either went up in the exchange or down, or the exchange is even. These relative terms refer to the point value of the pieces involved in the exchange. Here are some examples, all from white's perspective:

1. white captures a Bishop for a pawn (similar to what we saw above). The pawn is worth one point and the Bishop three, so white gave up one to gain three. This is up in the exchange by 2.

2. white captures a Knight for a Rook. This is down in the exchange because the Rook is worth five and the Knight is worth three, down by 2.

3. white captures a Knight for Bishop. The Knight and Bishop are both worth three, so this is an even exchange.
4. white captures a Rook and a Bishop (8 points) for a Knight and a Bishop (6 points), up by 2.

Even though new players know this, they will still make exchanges that cause them to go down in the exchange. You must remind your player often to ensure he understands when an exchange is bad for his side and when it is good for his side.

A strategy I tell my players to use is this: once you have gone up in an exchange, let's say something like a Rook for a Knight, or if you're up an entire piece, look for ways to start forcing your opponent to exchange his pieces away. In the end, you'll still be up the piece, and your opponent will not have a piece left. Keep in mind, however, that we are *always* on the lookout for checkmate.

Forcing the exchange is simply either you capture a piece with an equal valued piece, and your opponent must capture back or go farther down in the exchange; or to call check with a piece, forcing your opponent to capture, and you capture back.

Remind your player that once she's up in the exchange, every time she goes up in the exchange, or makes an even exchange, it's in her favor.

But wait! There's more!

Many books have been written on just the middle game, so I am not going to delve any farther into this part of the game. If you want to expand your, and / or your player's knowledge of the middle game, I recommend doing a search on www.amazon.com for "chess middle game." There will likely be 70 or 80 results. Read the reviews of the top few and order one. When it arrives, sit down at a table with a board and set and work through the examples and problems. Really, this is how you and your player become stronger players in the middle game. You can also do this with openings and the end game. Have fun studying!

I also recommend *Chess Life* magazine, and the website www.chessgames.com, where you can get great game analysis and games to study.

Lesson 8 – A complete game example

Now that we have a few chess weapons under our belt, let's go back to our game. You're going to play the opening from Lesson 6 again, but this time I'll comment on some of the moves (this is called annotation). Have your child help set up the board, and play with the white pieces.

1. e4   e5
2. Nf3   Nc6
3. Bb5   d6   with this move, black creates a pin on his own Knight with white's Bishop. Point this out.
4. Nc3   Bd7   here, black unpins the Knight.
5. d3   Nf6
6. Bg5 . . .   white creates another Bishop pin.
6. . . .   Be7   black undoes the pin.
7. 0-0   0-0

The rest of this game was created using Chessmaster 9000. If you'll forgive this digression, I want to talk briefly about the difference in play between an average chess player and a Grandmaster. The analogy I've always used is that the difference is like that between a Little League baseball player and a Major Leaguer. They're playing the same game, holding to the same rules, yet the way a grandmaster views the game is light years beyond the average player. Therefore: this game is between two slightly under the average players ("personalities" in Chessmaster 9000). This is to illustrate a game played the way players who are learning the game are going to play. In this way, we can examine the moves and identify errors in thinking and planning.

In the early stages of a player's chess career, some equally new opponents will make more, and obvious, mistakes. When a player learns to recognize an error, and can take advantage of it, the wins begin to follow. As a young player progresses and becomes more confidant and experienced, study of more advanced chess books is the next step.

For the rest of the game, we're going to switch our chess notation to the style that is standard in chess books and magazines. First comes the move number, the move for white, a space, then the move for black, followed by comments if any. The move numbers and moves are in **bold**, while alternative move choices in the comments are not in bold.

8. Bxf6 Bxf6 nothing wrong with this exchange. New players often exchange early and often, viewing it as a way to simplify things. **9. Nd5 . . .** white's Knight is now in black's territory. The d5 and e5 squares are often called outposts for the white Knights because they can strike deep into black's territory. The d4 and e4 squares are outposts for black's Knights. **9. . . . Kh8. 10. Bxc6 bxc6 11. Ne3 . . .** to escape the c pawn attack. **11. . . . Bh4** ask your player if the Bishop is a hung piece. Answer: no, the black Queen protects it. **12. Kh1 Bh3** ask if *this* Bishop is a hung piece. Answer: yes. **13. gxh3** capturing the Bishop. Now black is down a Bishop. The question now is whether white can take advantage. **13. . . . Qd7 14. Nxh4 Qxh3** trying to force something, but a Queen by herself is a lone piece. Remember combinations? Diagram next page.

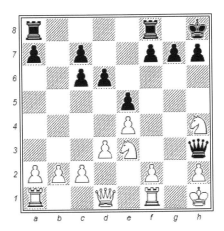

15. Qh5 . . . protects the Knight on h4. **15. . . . a6? 16. Ng4 . . .** advancing the Knight and also blocking off the black Queen from an escape route; there are no safe squares for her! Ask your player to look at all the squares and tell you why the queen cannot move there. Answers: All pieces the Queen *could* capture are protected. The vacant squares where she could move are all attacked by white (g2, the King; g3, the f and h pawns; f3, Knight on h4; e3, f pawn and Knight on g4) **16. . . . g5** thinking he can push the Knight out of the way. **17. Qxg5 f5** why not Rg8 attacking the Queen? **18. Nf6 . . .** escaping the pawn and closing in on the King. **18. . . . Rg8** a move late. **19. Qh6 . . .** ask your child if she sees the checkmate threat on black's King – Qxh7#.

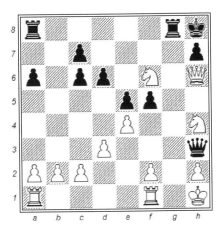

19. . . . Qxh4 stops the checkmate, but at great cost. Why didn't black play 19. . . . Rg7, protecting the checkmate square h7? It would have led to 20. Ng6+. Black would be forced to play 20. . . . Rxg6, then white 21. Qxh3 winning the Queen. **20. Qxh4** the end is near. **20. . . . Kg7** trying to avoid the mate by Qxh7. **21. Nxg8** a great exchange for white. **21. . . . Rxg8** this is better than Kxg8 because it brings the other Rook into play. **22. Rg1+** adding pressure. **22. . . . Kf7 23. Qxh7+ Kf6** hoping for safety amongst the pawns. **24. Qxg8 . . . fxe4** just doing something, anything. **25. Rg7** ignoring dxe4. Why bother, when mate is around the corner? **25. . . . exd3 26. Qf7# 1-0** (the "1-0" is the score of the game, white is listed first, so this shows a win for white. A black win would be "0-1" and a draw would be "½ - ½")

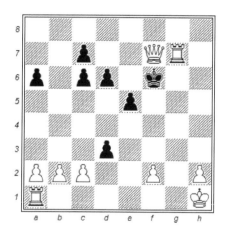

Have your child check each square the King *could* move to and tell you why he *cannot* move there. Ask him which piece prevents the King from moving to the square. For example: g6 – Rook and Queen attack the square; e7 – only the Queen. By the way, there are five squares.

There it is, a complete game, with all its strong and weak moves. Games between new players often have mates like this, and also you'll see early checkmates in less than twenty moves. So before we get into the end game, which is trademarked by few pieces on the board, we're going to move into what I lovingly call Lesson 9 – Early traps and checkmates.

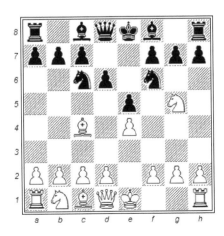

Lesson 9 – Early traps and checkmates

This lesson will help you teach your player some of the pitfalls that players like to try on an unsuspecting opponent.

Knight – Bishop attack

After the move 4. Ng5, the Knight is going to fork the Queen and Rook with the move Nxf7. We saw this fork earlier. This lesson shows how to defend against it.

If it's black's move, there is one best move for black. Ask your child try to find the solution presented here, d5,

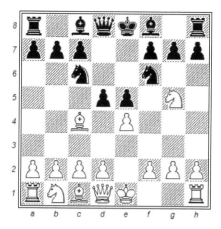

which typically leads to: **5. exd5 Nxd5 6. Bxd5 Qxd5** taking away the threat. Note that now, the black Queen threatens Qxg2. This would force white to castle to save the pawn.

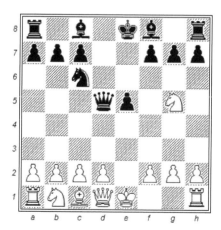

Four-move checkmate – Scholar's Mate

I am showing this checkmate so your child will learn how to *defend* against it, not how to *use* it. The problem is that young players often want to win so badly that this checkmate seems perfectly fair, and it is under the rules of chess, but a game that ends in four moves teaches nothing, and the players gain no valuable experience. I forbade my players from ever using it in a tournament, and not one of them did. They became stronger players for it. Play this through move three and ask your child if she can see the checkmate.

1. e4 e5 2. Bc4 Nc6 3. Qf3 d6

Note: Qf3 is the trademark move and black should be immediately on the alert for checkmate. Sometimes the Queen move is Qh5.

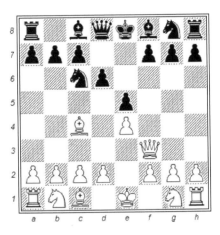

4. Qxf7#

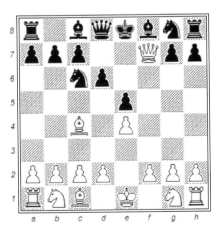

How do you defend against it? It's easy: **4. . . . Nf6**.

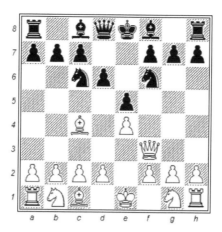

But what if the move is **4. Qh5** instead of **4. Qf3**? Does your child see a solution? Try **4. . . .g6**. Often, white will then move **5. Qf3**, as in the previous example. So black plays **5. . . . Nf6** and the attack completely fizzles with white moving the Queen twice, slowing piece development.

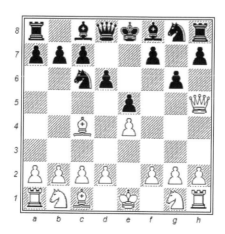

Lesson 10 – Is it really checkmate?

It's imperative that your child learns what is and isn't checkmate. In the next diagram, the move is **1. Qxg7#**. We have checkmate because she also attacks the only possible escape square – h8 – and is protected by the Knight on f5.

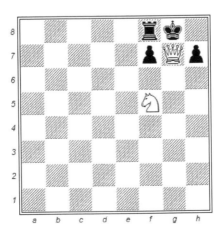

Let's look at a position that is not checkmate. In this position, the Rook is calling check by **1. Rxg7**, the same square the Queen was on, however, because the Rook attacks on files or rows, the King can now safely escape to h8.

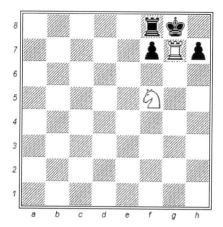

The best way to prevent your child from being "checkmated" when it is not really checkmate is to practice. Here are a couple of ideas you can try:

1. Set up several almost checkmates and have your child tell you whether it's really checkmate. For example, you can use the checkmate patterns from Lesson 5, but alter them by removing the piece that supports the piece calling check, or slightly change the position by having the attacker call check from a different square.

2. While playing games with your child, when the game reaches checkmate, whether on you or on him, ask him to prove that it is checkmate by showing that the attacking piece cannot be captured or blocked, and that the King cannot move to any square to escape.

Lesson 11 – End Game

I've saved the End Game for last, somehow that just seems fitting, and even though we've gone through a complete game, that example game didn't get into a true end game due to the checkmate on move 26, primarily due to the fact that there were quite a few pieces still on the board (note number 3 below).

The end game occurs when:

1. there has been no checkmate
2. many exchanges have taken place
3. there are few pieces left on the board.

There are many possibilities or "types" of ends games. On the next page is a list (not meant to be exhaustive, but representative) of the most common, especially in scholastic games. However, you can see that the list shows one side up (has more piece value) significantly in material. This is common in scholastic chess, at least when players are new to the game. Typically, one player achieves this advantage in the middle game. Remember, the way to win the game is through checkmate (or when the opponent resigns). Between two equal-strength players, checkmate rarely happens in the opening or middle game, and both players, while always on the lookout for mate, are also planning on how they want to be positioned for the end game.

1. King and two Rooks vs. King.
2. King, Queen and Rook vs. King.
3. King and Rook vs. King.
4. King and Queen vs. King.

First we'll discuss each of these four checkmates, then we'll examine Queening a pawn that has advanced to its 8th rank.

In each of the four checkmates we're going to visit, make sure your player understands each has a pattern of moves forcing the King into checkmate. These checkmates should be required and demonstrable (to you) knowledge before a player attends a tournament.

King and two Rooks vs. King

In this diagram, white has two Rooks that are ready to attack the black King. New players are always tempted to call check with one of the Rooks – either Ra6+, Re4+, Re3+, or Rg6+.

This is not the strongest move because you give your opponent choices. Instead, when you have two Rooks, you reduce your opponent's choices by using them together to herd the King to a side of the board, much like a Collie herding cattle toward the pen.

The first move is what I call "setting the perimeter" (or "fence") to cut off escape squares for the King, in effect, reducing the King's options. In the position on the previous page, the move could be either Ra5 or Rg5. My preferred choice is Ra5.

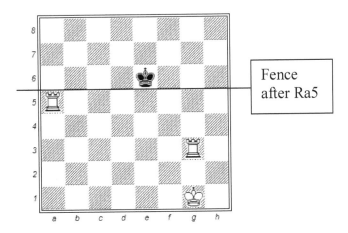

Fence after Ra5

Why is this? If we move Rg5, the black King can attack that Rook on its next move by Kf6. True, the Rook can run away to Rb5 (not a5, as that would block off the a-file Rook), but this is a wasted move and if your player is in time trouble, seconds matter. Once we have set the perimeter (fence), it's time to call check. Here's our checkmate in action from the beginning:

1. Ra5 Kd6 2. Rg6+ Ke7 3. Ra7+ Kf8:

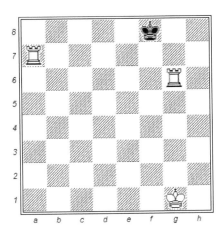

RONN MUNSTERMAN

We can't blindly move our Rook to g8+. Why not? The King will simply capture it. What to do? We run the Rook away. But note that we don't put it on the same file as the other Rook (a). This is part of the pattern your player must recognize – Rooks are always on the diagonal to each other when they are close to each other, but never, ever on the same file or row. So we have **4. Rb6 Ke8**:

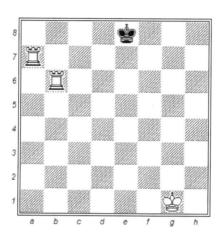

To finish off the black King: **5. Rb8#**:

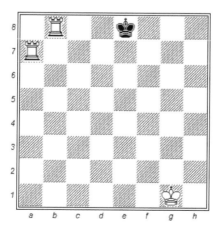

King, Queen and Rook vs. King

This checkmate can be accomplished in a way similar to the two Rook checkmate.

This position occurs after c8 = Q (the pawn moved to the 8th rank and was promoted to Queen).

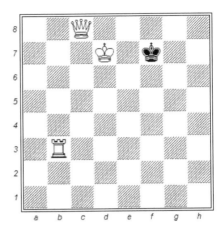

1. Qe8+ setting the perimeter – the King is restricted to moving to either g7 or f6. Most players opt for moving toward the center of the board: **1. . . . Kf6 2. Rf3+** now that the perimeter is already set by the Queen, the Rook can fire away with check. **2. . . . Kg5 3. Qg8+ Kh4** We can't move Rh3+ because the King can capture it, so we run the Rook away with **4. Rf7 Kh5 5. Rh7#.**

See the pattern? There are other ways to checkmate with a Queen and a Rook, but I found that for new players, once they learn the pattern for the two Rooks, and use that when they have a Queen and a Rook, they are already comfortable and able to win the "won" game.

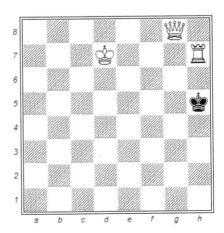

RONN MUNSTERMAN

King and Rook vs. King

This is a pattern different from the two checkmates we just examined. It requires more precise play (moves) by the player with the Rook. It is a checkmate that must be practiced often to fully understand the principles. The two principles are:

1. setting the perimeter (which we just discussed)
2. using the King to gain opposition.

Opposition occurs when the two Kings are facing each other, with one empty square between them. Remember, Kings can never be on squares next to each other, that's illegal. But there's a little more to it: the King who moves *into* the position creates opposition, and is said to be "in opposition." When we have the Rook, we do not want to create opposition, we want our *opponent* to create opposition.

First let's look at Kings in opposition:

If the black King just moved to e7, then he is in opposition. If it was the white's move and he moved to e5, he is in opposition. This tells us that we must know whose turn it was (or is) to be able to determine which King is in opposition. Explain to your child again, for emphasis, the Kings cannot be on squares next to each other. In this case, neither King can move to d6, e6, or f6. It is important to understand that Kings can block each other from moving to certain squares.

Let's see how this knowledge helps us when we're trying to checkmate with a Rook and King. In this position, the Rook has already set the perimeter, cutting off the 6th rank from the black King. The importance of this position is fundamental to checkmate with a King and Rook: if the Kings are in opposition and the player with the Rook has the move, the Rook can call check safely.

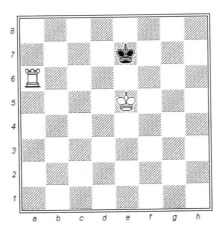

It's time to call check: Ra7+. The black King moves to d8, toward the Rook:

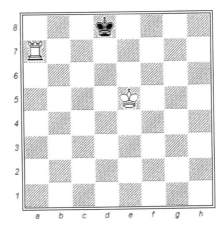

Now what does white do? If we move Ra8+, the black King can just escape (jumping our fence) back to the 7th rank, such as to c7. This is something we don't want because it will cost us more time and effort. What if we move our white King to e6? What will the sequence look like? Let's find out: **1.Ke6 Kc8** because if the black King moves to e8 and into opposition, then 2. Ra8#. **2. Kd6 Kb8** (attacks the Rook) **3. Rh7** (run as far as possible) **3. . . . Ka8**:

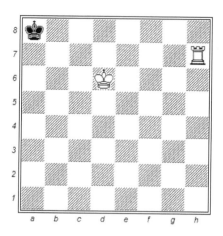

After **4. Kc6 Kb8**.

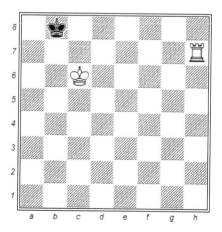

Now we have a situation to think about. Remember, we want the black King to create opposition (c8 in this position) so we can call checkmate on the 8th rank with the Rook. However, if we create opposition by moving **5. Kb6**, black will move **5. . . . Kc8** (breaking opposition) and we're back to having to chase the King down again. How do we avoid this? There's a lovely chess term for exactly this position:

Zwischenzug, German for "in-between move." In our position, we don't want to move the King and we don't want to call check by moving 5. Rh8+. Our solution? We make a move that has no real effect on our position, but forces black to move into a worse position (another German word: *zugzwang*, "compulsion to move.") We burn the move by **5. Rg7**.

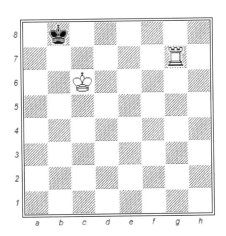

This forces black to move **5. . . . Ka8**, followed by **6. Kb6 Kb8** (no other choice now and creates opposition) **7. Rg8#**.

Be sure your child fully understands that this is checkmate because the white King blocks all three squares (a7, b7, and c7) that the black King needs to escape the Rook's check.

One way to provide a fun way to practice this (or other end game checkmates) is to time your player and challenge him to do it faster each time.

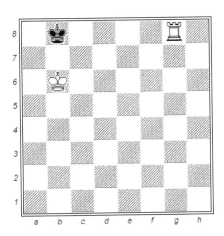

King and Queen vs. King

In this position, the Queen's first responsibility is to force the black King to an edge of the board. Note that none of the Queen's moves call check until the very end when it's checkmate.

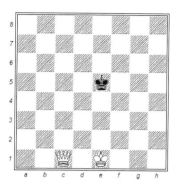

1. Qc4, note that the Queen is a Knight's move away from the black King.

This is the necessary pattern to use. It forces the black King to make a choice that will always push him closer to the edge. Look closely and you'll see the pattern emerge. **1. . . . Kf5 2.Qd4**

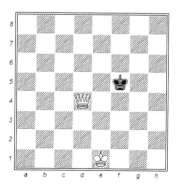

2. . . . Ke6 3.Qc5 Kf6 4.Qd5 Ke7 5.Qc6 Kf7 6.Qd6 Ke8 7.Qc7 Kf8 8.Qd7 Kg8 9.Qe7 Kh8.

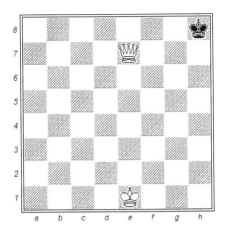

In the above position, the Queen can move no closer to the black King, otherwise he will be stalemated – no squares to legally move to! This would be throwing away a win and getting only one-half point for white. Make sure your child understands stalemate. You may have to go over it many times periodically.

Now we bring up the white King: **10.Kf2 Kg8 11.Kg3 Kh8 12.Kg4 Kg8 13.Kg5 Kh8 14.Kg6 Kg8 15.Qe8#.** Point out that the Queen could have moved **15. Qg7#.**

The keys to remember are: don't call check with the Queen until checkmate, and avoid stalemate by leaving an escape square, while bringing the King up to help.

Queening a pawn

Kids love the idea of getting a Queen for a pawn! The trick is learning how to go about it in a situation where the player has only the pawn and a King, and is playing against a single King. There are two key points to Queening a pawn:

1. the opposing King and the "rule of the square"
2. opposition (which we discussed earlier).

This is a tough skill to teach and to learn. It takes practice, lot's of it, to learn whether the player with the pawn can actually get it to the Queening square safely. First, we'll look at "rule of the square" to see whether a player needs to use his King to protect the pawn and the Queening square.

Rule of the square

Simply put, the question is whether the opposing King can catch the lone pawn before it can safely Queen itself. The square is determined this way: in this position we create the square by following the diagonal from the pawn to the 8th rank. It ends on b8. We draw a line down until we are on the same rank as the pawn – 4th rank, or b4. The square f8 is the Queening square and it completes the square.

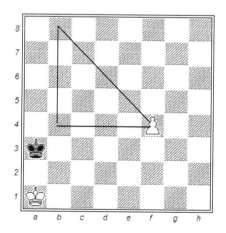

The "rule of the square" says that if the King is inside the square, he can catch the pawn, or if he's outside the square, but it's his move and can move *into* the square, he can catch the pawn. If he's not inside the square, the pawn will safely Queen in time. So in this position, if it's white's move, the pawn will Queen, but if it's black's move he can move inside the square to b4 and catch the pawn.

The best way for your player to see this is to set it up and play it. Have white move first: **1. f5 Kb4 2. f6 Kc5 3. f7 Kd6 4. f8=Q+.** Do you see that the King is two squares away from the new Queen and cannot capture her, plus it's check?

Now for black to move first: **1. . . . Kb4 2.f5 Kc5 3. f6 Kd6 4. f7 Ke7. 5. f8=Q+**, black can simply capture the unprotected new Queen **5. . . . Kxf8**, which creates a King vs. King draw. Also note that in this position, white's King cannot get to the pawn first to protect it, even if he moves first – the black King is always in position to head him off.

RONN MUNSTERMAN

Opposition

In our earlier checkmate example of a King and a Rook against a lone King, we wanted our opponent to create opposition so we could move the Rook to call check, thus forcing the King to retreat closer to an edge of the board. When trying to advance a pawn, *we* want to create opposition ourselves to control the squares in front of the pawn.

If the rule of the square shows that the pawn cannot get to the Queening square by itself, the King must get in position to protect *both* the pawn and the Queening square. This gets more complicated, but we'll try to illustrate some points that will help your player understand what's required of the King. In this position, white has just moved **1. Kc5** which gains (or creates) the opposition.

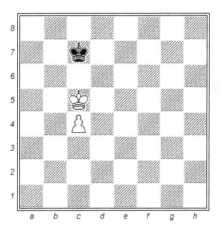

Now black must surrender the opposition by moving either backwards or to one side: **1. . . . Kd7 2. Kb6 Kc8** – the Queening square. **3. Kc6** gaining the opposition again **3. . . . Kd8** losing the opposition. **4. Kb7** protecting the Queening square **4. . . . Kd7 5. c5 Kd8 6. c6 Ke7** (note that now the black King is running away).

7.c7 Kf6 8. c8=Q. Now the game becomes a King and Queen vs. King and is a won game for white.

RONN MUNSTERMAN

Lesson 12 – Thinking, Chess Calculations

Chess is entirely a thinking game. Accurate analysis of the current position *and* the possibilities that can be derived from it (variations) are central to winning chess. This section covers how to teach your child to think like a winning chess player. We've examined the three parts of the game, the opening, middle, and end games, and a complete game of twenty-six moves. Now it's time to learn what the thought process should be during each and every move.

You're asking, "How does this work?" We begin by using a list of things a player must ask herself *before* moving. Note the emphasis on "before." I call this the Golden Four (questions). New players who learn to do this out of habit will become stronger players for it, and will begin to win more games.

The Golden Four

1. What checks can you call?
2. What captures can you make?
3. What checks can your opponent call?
4. What captures can your opponent make?

The best way to teach this is to start a game, play through the opening. When that's accomplished, both you and your child run through each of the four questions when it's your turn *out loud*. Since this is a teaching game, neither of you is going to be giving away state secrets of your plan. Play several games like this.

Then it's time to move back to mental thinking.

How do you know whether your player is getting used to this and is actually doing it? If she's no longer hanging pieces (Lesson 7), she's doing it more often than not.

The Platinum Ten

If we expand on the Golden Four, we get another list of things for a player to consider. Teaching this thought process will take longer, but I recommend doing the same *thinking out loud* process you and your child used for the Golden Four. After a new player begins to think like this regularly, he will become an even stronger player.

1. Can I call check?
2. Would it be checkmate?
3. What pieces (of my opponent) can I capture?
4. Are the pieces that can be captured protected? This is looking for hanging pieces.
5. Where can I move my pieces? (Meaning empty squares)
6. Can my opponent call check?
7. Would it be checkmate?
8. What pieces (of mine) can my opponent capture?
9. Are the pieces that can be captured protected? This is looking for hanging pieces.
10. Where can my opponent move her pieces? (Meaning empty squares)

"If I, then he" move pairs

Chess players often talk about how "deep" they can see moves. What they mean is how many moves in a particular sequence can they "see" and understand, and, more importantly, visualize the board's position after the sequence would be finished. Another way of putting this thought process is that a player will say to himself, "If I move there, he'll do this, then I'll move this," etc. The more "if I, then he" calculations there are, the deeper the player is seeing the sequence. Most experienced chess players (and by this, I generally mean those who've played under tournaments conditions) will say they can comfortably see about four or five moves deep. This really means ten moves, because they are referring to "if I, then he" pairs of moves as one move in their count.

To illustrate this "if I, then he" idea, let's look at a position from a game I played in a 2010 tournament. This game also appears on page 114 as a sample game. The position occurs after **13. . . . Bxe4?** This move was a blunder on its own (a Bishop for a pawn), but rather than just capture back with Nxe4, I looked at other possibilities. I was wondering whether I could get his Queen or Rook into a position where I could fork the Queen or Rook by attacking in a specific order.

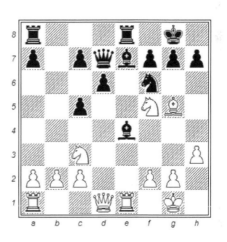

What I was thinking was: If I move **14. Nxe7+**, then he plays **Rxe7**, I play **15. Bxf6,** then he plays **gxf6,** I play **16. Nxe4** attacking the f6 pawn. If he plays **Rae8,** then I play **17. Nxf6+** after which he resigned due to the royal fork. I grant you that there were other options for black, and I considered them, but left them out of this thought string to keep it simple. The diagram on the next page shows how it turned out.

After 17. Nxf6+!

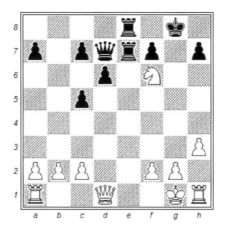

Note that if instead of **14 . . . Rxe7**, he had played **14 . . . Qxe7**, it would have gone like this: **15. Bxf6 Qxf6 16. Rxe4**, and I'd have been up in material by a Bishop.

See Ahead Score Sheet

We'll cover keeping score in Chapter 16, but I wanted to provide this score sheet here. After you have taught your player how to keep score, and you are ready to expand a little more on the move calculations thought process, you can use the score sheet on the next page.

Let's say your son is playing white. The way it works is that after you play through the opening, you ask your player (for each move) to write down in the column labeled 1 for white the move he is considering. Next, is to write down what he thinks you will move in column 1 for black. He should repeat for move 2 and 3 in that planned sequence. Tell him that this is chess calculation, but it is on paper. He should get all three move pairs written, then plays his first move of the sequence. For every move of yours that he "predicts" he gets a point. You do the same. Keep track of the points and whoever has the most after, say, ten moves, wins that contest.

It's important that after playing this a couple of times, you play regular games without the See Ahead Score Sheet.

See Ahead Score Sheet

Move	White	Black	1 W	1 B	2 W	2 B	3 W	3 B
1								
2								
3								
4								
5								
6								
7								
8								
9								
10								
11								
12								
13								
14								
15								
16								
17								
18								
19								
20								

Important note: The See Ahead Score Sheet is not allowed in tournaments due to a rule that a player must make the move first, then record it.

Lesson 13 – Touch-move

This is just what it sounds like. There are two parts to the rule that become especially important with new players:

1. The essence of the rule is that if you touch a piece and it's reasonable to believe you intend to move it, you must move it, *if it can be moved legally.*
2. However, a move is not complete until the player lets go of the piece. What this means is that a player may pick up a piece, put it down on an empty square (but not let go), see that it's really a weak move, and place it on another square, then release the piece.

The touch-move rule also applies to the instance where a player touches an opponent's piece in an obvious intent to capture it. The player must capture the piece if he can legally capture it. By this, we mean that sometimes a player just makes a mistake thinking he can capture a piece, when he cannot. In this case, the "touch" does not count. Another point to make is that some players pick up their piece first, and place it on the square where the to-be-captured piece sits, and touch the opponent's piece with their capturing piece. This is a touch-move situation.

When playing a casual game, players often relax this rule, but it's best to make sure both players know the rule has been set aside.

All tournament play, and chess club games that "count," such as Club Ladder games (See page 175) are touch-move.

When you think your child is ready for touch-move, introduce it, but be willing to relax it, too, including take-back moves.

Hovering – the helicopter hand

When the touch-move rule is introduced, new players are prone to do one or both of these things:

1. While deciding what move to make, they hover their hand over the board like a helicopter, swooping first toward one piece, then another, then eventually touch the piece they (hopefully) intend to move.
2. After moving a piece, a player will perch his finger on the top of the piece and then try to look at the board often moving his hand around, but still touching the piece, to see if the move is really safe.

If your child begins to exhibit either of these bad habits, discourage him immediately. I tell my players to keep their hands on their lap, even sit on them if they have to, and not to bring a hand near the board until they have made their decision on which piece to move.

Remind your player that he needs to be able to "see" what the board will look like after the move – *in his head*!

Lesson 14 – Tips for playing a student

Take back moves

While teaching your student to play, I encourage the take-back move. This is where, if you see your player has made a weak move, suggest he take the move back and look for a stronger one. You must also immediately explain why the move is weak. The purpose of the take-back move is not to let your player win the game, but rather prolong it, providing more playing experience. If a new player only makes it to move 20 when playing, how will he learn to finish a game?

Odds chess

This is a way to alter the board to even the game between you and your child. The idea is simple: before playing, *you* take a piece off the board, thereby giving your child a position of being "up" in material from the very beginning. Start with the Queen, then as your child gets stronger, you start reducing the odds: Rook, Bishop or Knight, pawn. I recommended that you do this sparingly, however, and rely also on the take-back moves, so your child sees a complete board and all the complications that come with it more often than not.

Time odds chess

If you have a chess clock and have introduced your child to it already, you can set the clocks differently, giving your child more time than you have. If you're not familiar with chess clocks, don't worry, we'll discuss them in Chapter 15.

Lesson 15 – Chess Clocks

Time flies when you're having fun

The next two Lessons (15 and 16) are on the clock and keeping score. Experience taught me that it's best for the player to first introduce the clock and play a number of games with it to let him get used to playing with it. Take the clock away and work on Lesson 16 – Keeping Score. Play some games with him so he can practice keeping score. Once you've done that, bring back the clock and play games with both the clock and scorekeeping.

The chess clock is used in a way similar to a clock in a football or basketball game. When time runs out in those games, the game is over and the team with the most points wins. In chess, we measure the amount of time a player uses to make his moves, which measures "thinking" time.

A chess clock is actually two clocks in the same plastic, metal, or wood body, one for each player. When Player A (white) is making a move, his clock is running and his opponent's clock is stopped. After Player A completes the move on the board, he pushes or "hits" his clock – a button or lever that will start Player B's clock and stop his own.

An important thing to note is the time is never so much time per one move, it is always so much time for all moves, or as we'll see shortly, a specified number of moves within a certain time.

There are two kinds of clocks – analog, which is like a round clock on the wall with hour and minute hands, and digital, which counts down from a specified amount of time, such as 30 minutes.

As the game progresses, the players' clocks run down or approach the end time (on the analog this is 6:00 for the first time period, if there are more than one, then 7:00, 8:00 and so on). When time runs out for one player (this is called Sudden Death), he has lost the game on time *if* his opponent has *mating material*, which can include a single pawn with the King. Certain pieces cannot complete checkmate with only a King, so if the opponent has a King and *one* of these pieces, the game is a draw (a tie) by rule:

- Bishop
- Knight

Even if the player whose clock runs out has more material on the board, he still loses the game. Read Chapter 8 – A short rules list for tournament players or the *Official Rules of Chess* for more on rules.

When introducing the clock to your child, be aware of two things:

1. the clock is a deadline device and that brings with it a certain amount of tension, especially for a new player. Tell your child that everyone is on the clock, so it's not just them, and that everyone at a tournament will be feeling nervous just as they are – there are no exceptions!

2. new players often forget to hit their clock to stop it and start their opponent's clock. Be sure to remind your child when you are playing with him to hit the clock – it's a habit that must be developed.

To get started, you must first decide what amount of time to use. I'd suggest something like ten or fifteen minutes. This may seem rather quick to you, but for the purpose of learning to play with the clock, it'll work out just fine. Of course, if you really prefer, use a longer time period. Set your clocks and start playing.

By the way, if you bought a digital clock, and have never used one before, you are probably going to have to read the instructions on setting the clock. Really.

Time frames used in chess

There are many time frames, or the amount of time available for each player. Here's a short list of the most common. All times are considered to be Sudden Death unless so noted. Times are shown using "G" for game. For example, a time of G/30, means Sudden Death with a time of 30 minutes for each player. All times that are less than 30 minutes are called "Quick chess."

G/5   Speed chess
G/15
G/30   Action chess
G/45
G/60
40/90, SD60 – must make 40 moves in 90 minutes, then it's Sudden Death in an additional 60 minutes.

Playing with a clock

1. Set up the board.
2. Set the clock. For example on an analog, for a fifteen minute game, you set the clocks at 5:45. On a digital, you select the time frame of G/15.
3. If the clock is analog and is a "wind-up" type, not battery powered, be sure it is wound up, but be careful not to over-wind it.
4. Place the clock by the board. By rule, the black player gets to decide which side of the board the clock sits on, unless he is late to the game. Most players will put the clock on the same side as they are "handed." A right-handed player will put the clock on his right. This puts the clock on the left side for a right-handed white player and forces that player to either move left-handed, or cross over with his right hand to hit the clock.

5. The black player pushes the button or lever that starts white's clock.
6. White moves and "hits" his clock using the same hand he moved with. This is by rule.
7. Black moves and "hits" his clock using the same hand he moved with.
8. Continue through the rest of the game.

Your child may forget to hit his clock, just remind him. It's a habit that must be developed through practice. I recommend that you play several games, maybe even ten to fifteen games over a period of a week or so using the clock before moving on to Lesson 16 – Keeping Score.

Time delay clocks

Digital clocks introduced the capability of adding a "delay" to the time. What this means is that if the time delay is five seconds (most common), the clock waits five seconds to start counting down. The purpose is to avoid a scramble to move, because the player will always have at least the five seconds to move.

Lesson 16 – Keeping Score (writing chess notation)

Keeping score means to record all moves made by *both* players, typically on a piece of paper, called a score sheet, although there are specialized electronic devices that can be used in place of paper. A score sheet may be pre-printed, have a carbon-like second copy, or may be in a book. Most players prefer to use a book (typically 50 games) so they can always go back and examine or study a game. On page 112 is a blank sample score sheet.

On the score sheet, there are places for information about the tournament, players' names and ratings (if they have one) and the results and signature line. The bulk of the score sheet is used to record the move made by each player. Each player must record his *and* his opponent's move. On page 114 is a sample game score sheet.

A recent rule change requires that the player *first* makes the move on the board, *then* writes it down on the score sheet, not the other way around. This is due to a rule that forbids the use of any kind of memory aid. While there are proponents to writing the move first then making it on the board, any argument is irrelevant because the current rule is clear. Move first, then write.

RONN MUNSTERMAN

One thing I highly recommend for new players is for them to literally sit on their hands to prevent them from making a knee-jerk-reaction kind of move, the kind that often leads to lost games. This forces them to be slow to react to a threatening move and allows them to examine the position more deeply, perhaps finding a solution to the threat or a bigger threat that they can make – like Mate! I will also say that if a player gets into time trouble, which means his clock's time is running out, he may have to make reaction moves. If this is the case, then experience counts heavily.

Here again from Lesson 4 – Reading Chess Notation are the symbols used:

Piece	Symbol
King	K
Queen	Q
Rook	R
Bishop	B
Knight	N
pawn	file letter

Action	Symbol
Capture	x
Check	+
Checkmate	# or ++
Castle-Kingside	O-O
Castle-Queenside	O-O-O
Pawn promotion	=

Comments on a move

! a particularly good (and usually surprising) move
!! an excellent move
? a bad move
?? a blunder
!? an interesting move that may not be best
?! a dubious move - one which may turn out to be bad

Blank Score sheet

Event:			Date:		
White:			Rating:		
Black:			Rating:		
Round:			Board:		
	White	Black		White	Black
1			26		
2			27		
3			28		
4			29		
5			30		
6			31		
7			32		
8			33		
9			34		
10			35		
11			36		
12			37		
13			38		
14			39		
15			40		
16			41		
17			42		
18			43		
19			44		
20			45		
21			46		
22			47		
23			48		
24			49		
25			50		

White won   Black won   Draw

Opponent's Signature _____

Recording the moves

Sometimes, two of the same kind of piece can move to the same square. In order to make sure that our scorekeeping is clear, we use a method to identify the moving piece by where it started from. In this diagram, white's two Rooks can both move to the same square, e5. If the Rook on e1 is moved to e5, we would write R1e5 (Rook on 1 to e5). If it was the other Rook, we would write R5e5. We could also write Ree5 and Rae5.

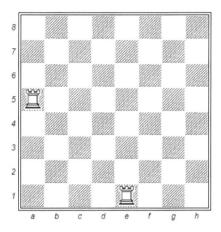

Let's take a look at a sample score sheet of a short game. The score sheet is on the next page.

White moves his pawn to e4. After moving, he will write "e4" on his score sheet on the line for move 1 under the White column and Black will do the same. Black will make his move and write it down, in this case, "e5" and white will, too. Both players are required to write down moves by *both* players. Read through, and play the game on a board with your player. See if your board matches the one on page 115.

Sample Game Score sheet

	White	Black		White	Black
Event: Leatherjackets			Date: 2/6/2010		
White: Ronn			Rating:		
Black: Robert			Rating:		
Round: 2			Board: 11		
1	e4	e5	26		
2	Nf3	Nc6	27		
3	Bb5	d6	28		
4	Bxc6	bxc6	29		
5	h3	Nf6	30		
6	d3	Be7	31		
7	Nc3	O-O	32		
8	O-O	Re8	33		
9	Re1	Bb7	34		
10	d4	exd4	35		
11	Nxd4	c5	36		
12	Nf5	Qd7	37		
13	Bg5	Bxe4?	38		
14	Nxe7+	Rxe7	39		
15	Bxf6	gxf6	40		
16	Nxe4	Rae8	41		
17	Nxf6+!!	Resign	42		
18			43		
19			44		
20			45		
21			46		
22			47		
23			48		
24			49		
25			50		

(White won)   Black won   Draw

Opponent's Signature *Robert Johnson*

Position of sample game score sheet following 17. Nxf6+!!
Remember what the "!!" means? Excellent move. You'll see that
the Knight has forked black's King, Queen, and Rook; the royal
fork! This is why black resigned. Does your board match the
diagram?

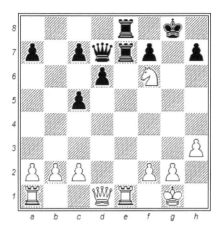

At the bottom of the score sheet I circled "White won" and
had my opponent sign it to prove he agrees with the circled
outcome. This can become important if there is a later dispute
over the result of the game.

It's time to practice keeping score. You can either photocopy
the blank score sheet on page 112, or use a score book or just
plain paper. Whatever you choose, begin.

Play a game, with you and your child recording the moves.
Tell your child that he should ask you for help if he isn't sure
what to write. You can talk to each other, saying for example,
"Okay, I moved Knight to f3, so I write that as Nf3." When the
game is over, reset the board and play the game through like you
did with my sample game. This is when you may discover errors
in the scorekeeping. Correct the mistakes, and try to make it all
the way through the game.

Repeat this exercise several times together. You should see a
decrease in the number of scorekeeping questions. When you
feel your child has gotten at least a little comfortable with
keeping score, it's time to bring back the clock.

Tying together the clock and score sheet

When using the clock and score sheet together for the first time, some new players may feel overwhelmed. It just seems like so much to remember and do: think, move, hit the clock, write the move. So we practice. Tip: players should hit the clock, then write while their opponent's clock is running.

Have everything ready. Set the clock, perhaps a longer timeframe, like G/30. Before you start, both of you should write your names on the score sheet and the date. When you're both ready, black hits the clock and off you go. Play several games using the clock and keeping score over a period of time. The more your child plays this way, the better he'll become at it, and he'll soon be able to do it without it being "something extra" to have to do. It becomes just a part of the game.

Exceptions

When playing in a tournament, keeping score is required, with a few exceptions. Tournament directors can, at their discretion, waive the rule either for all players, or on a case by case basis, and for example, some scholastic directors waive it for players who have not learned to keep score before coming to the tournament. The caveat usually given by these directors, though, is that if a player does not keep score, he gives up the right to certain claims such as draw on triple occurrence of position (See Chapter 8.)

Keeping all of this in mind, I always insisted that my players knew how to keep score before attending a tournament.

Special rule

When keeping score and using a clock, when one of the players' clock hits five minutes to go, *both* players may, if they choose to, stop keeping score. *Both* players are allowed to ask another person to keep score for them (usually a friend or teammate). They should stop the clock first.

Part Two – The Chess World

$$\text{♟ ♜ ♞ ♝ ♛ ♚}$$

Chapter 1 – The Chess World

By the chess world I mean those people and things who play and / or support chess. Some examples are chess organizations, chess magazines, chess officials, chess coaches, and the players, both amateur and professional, including world champions.

There many chess organizations in the United States. Here are some of the most well-known:

- The United States Chess Federation (USCF).
- State Chess organizations.
- Military Chess clubs.
- Local Chess clubs.
- Collegiate Chess clubs.
- Scholastic chess clubs.

Outside the United States, each country may have its own governing body or organization. For example, in England the organization is the British Chess Federation, which like the USCF, is affiliated with the World Chess Federation, also called Fédération Internationale des Échecs (FIDE, pronounced fee-day). FIDE is the governing body which confers titles and conducts the tournaments for the world champion titles. See page 121, Chess Titles and Ratings.

In this chapter, I will be focusing on the United States, but if you are in another country, an internet search will help you locate the governing chess body(ies) for your location.

United States Chess Federation (USCF)

The USCF celebrated its 70th anniversary in 2009. You can find information about the USCF at www.uschess.org. Below, I have included information from its web site. USCF membership is required to play in USCF rated tournaments. See the web site for membership rates. Scholastic discounts are available.

From their web site:

The United States Chess Federation (USCF) is the official, not-for-profit US membership organization for chess players and chess supporters of all ages and strengths, from beginners to Grandmasters. The USCF represents the United States in the World Chess Federation (FIDE), linking US members to chess players around the world. Founded in 1939 with the merger of the American Chess Federation and the National Chess Federation to promote the, USCF has grown to over 80,000 members and 2,000+ affiliated chess clubs and organizations today. Under the management of a professional staff headquartered in Crossville, Tennessee, USCF sanctions thousands of tournaments with over half a million officially rated games annually. 25 National Championships award titles to both amateurs and professionals, ranging from elementary school students to senior citizens. Over fifty Grandmasters (one out of every eight GMs in the world) represent the US internationally, and USCF supports the participation of Americans in official FIDE championship events at all levels.

USCF publishes the award-winning monthly magazine Chess Life, the bimonthly Chess Life for Kids, and this extensive and feature-rich web site. We welcome you to read our mission statement, learn about the benefits of membership, and to join with chess players and fans from throughout the US, in greater enjoyment of "the royal game."

USCF Mission Statement

USCF is a not-for-profit membership organization devoted to extending the role of chess in American society.

USCF promotes the study and knowledge of the game of chess, for its own sake as an art and enjoyment, but also as a means for the improvement of society. It informs, educates, and fosters the development of players (professional and amateur) and potential players. It encourages the development of a network of institutions devoted to enhancing the growth of chess, from local clubs to state and regional associations, and it promotes chess in American schools.

To these ends, USCF offers a monthly magazine, as well as targeted publications to its members and others. It supervises the organization of the U.S. chess championship, an open tournament every summer, and other national events. It offers a wide range of books and services to its members and others at prices consistent with the benefit of its members.

USCF serves as the governing body for chess in the United States and as a participant in international chess organizations and projects. It is structured to ensure effective democratic procedures in accord with its bylaws and the laws of the state of Illinois.

The USCF publishes a monthly magazine, *Chess Life*, and a bi-monthly magazine for kids, aptly named *Chess Life for Kids*. I recommend that you as the parent or coach, join USCF to get the adult magazine to strengthen your own game and to keep up with the chess world news, and to be able to find tournament listings. I also recommend that you consider getting a membership for the kids magazine for your child (or coaches, suggest this to your players' parents).

I've been a USCF member since 1987, with a few years off here and there. After my first tournament, my provisional rating was 1087, having won two games out of five. See page 121 for more on ratings. When my son was about nine, I started paying double annual fees for ten years so he would be a Life member, which he enjoys as an adult.

The USCF website has many nice features. Among them is a player search to see what someone's rating is or your own, plus it'll give you a complete tournament history going back to about 1992. There are other great resources for all players, especially scholastics.

State Organizations

Most states have a chess association which can be found by searching the internet for "Your state name" plus "chess association." These organizations are affiliated with the USCF and most provide support and information about scholastic chess for their state. The state organization typically acts as the clearinghouse for chess tournaments that are held in that state, thus providing a one-place-to-look type of service when you are searching for tournaments in a particular state.

State organizations are typically incorporated and have a constitution and / or bylaws that govern how they operate. They will likely have a board of directors (elected by the members) and officers (members of the board, elected by the board) such as:

- President
- Vice-president
- Secretary
- Treasure
- Executive Director
- Membership coordinator
- Tournament Coordinator
- State magazine editor
- Scholastic coordinator.

All state organizations have one thing in common with each other and with the USCF: to promote chess in their state, for both adult and scholastic players. This will often be their mission statement similar to the one for the USCF.

Many state organizations publish a magazine with information about chess in that state. Typically, when you become a member you automatically receive the magazine. Some states do like the USCF (with *Chess Life*) and provide a choice to view the magazine online (sometimes as an Adobe .pdf file) instead of receiving it in the mail, to save costs.

Chess Clubs

Chess clubs play an important role in a chess player's life. They provide a place where he can go play a game just for fun, make new friends, hang out with old ones, and have fun around a favorite game. Many clubs have a long history, like the Marshall Chess Club in New York City. This is where some of the best players in American chess history have played, and perhaps got their start as young men and women chess players. Their web site is www.marshallchessclub.org.

To find a chess club in your area, you can go to www.uschess.org and click the link for Clubs and Tourneys, click Chess Clubs, click your state name. Another way is to find your state chess organization as noted above, and look for a link for Clubs.

Some chess clubs affiliate with the USCF and those are the ones that will be listed on the site www.uschess.org. Generally, clubs affiliate with the USCF so they can conduct USCF rated tournaments, and to be listed on the USCF web site.

Chess Titles and Ratings

Ratings are earned by playing another rated player in a rated tournament. A rated tournament means that the results of the tournament are sent to the USCF (nowadays electronically) and the USCF runs its rating program for each player, calculating each player's new rating. All USCF members' ratings are stored with the USCF and available online. As of this writing, the records online go back to 1992.

When a player first plays in a "rated" tournament, he is considered to be "unrated." Until he has played twenty tournament games, his rating is called "Provisional" and is shown like this: P/games played. For example, if Bill played five games in his first tournament, his rating could appear like this: 1024 P/5. After the twenty tournament games, the player then becomes "rated," and the provisional tag is dropped.

A chess rating is a record of a player's past performance. It measures several things at once in its calculation (which is a rather complicated algorithm) and provides a number. This number is a player's rating. In a way that's similar to golfers and bowlers who ask "What's your handicap?" or "What's your average?" respectively, chess players ask, "What's your rating?"

The rating is a measure of relative strength as a player, and the higher, the stronger.

Without going into all of the math, I will say that the difference in rating points between two players on any given day, will be a statistical predictor of the winner. For two players who are nearly equal in rating, say 1500 versus a 1480, the statistics show that each player has a 50-50 chance of winning. However, as I told my players and the little league ball players I coached, stats are only that, and a well prepared player (or team) will often perform above their stats and that's why we play the game, rather than just sit around and compare our stats!

Ratings are broken down into titles and classes. As mentioned earlier, titles are awarded by the World Chess Federation (FIDE) and in the United States, classes are broken down by the ratings system used by the USCF. Below are the titles and the FIDE rating, followed by the USCF classes and their ratings.

- Grandmaster (GM) – title awarded by FIDE for GM norms * (next page)
- International Master (IM) – title awarded by FIDE for IM norms
- FIDE Master (FM) – minimum FIDE rating of 2300 after 24 games
- National Senior Master (SM) – USCF 2400+
- National Master (Master or NM) – USCF Master – USCF 2200+
- USCF Expert – USCF 2000+
- National Class A (USCF 1800- 1999) – top amateur class
- National Class B (USCF 1600-1799) – above average tournament player
- National Class C (USCF 1400-1599) – average tournament player
- National Class D (USCF 1200-1399) – a strong social player
- National Class E (USCF 1000-1199) – social / scholastic players
- National Class F (USCF 800-999) – novice / scholastic players

- National Class G (USCF 600-799) – beginner II/scholastic players
- National Class H (USCF 400-599) – beginner I / scholastic players
- National Class I (USCF 200-399) – early beginner / scholastic players
- National Class J (USCF 100-199) – minimum rating

* Grandmaster and International master candidates must play in three or more Norm events, which usually means to play grandmasters or international masters and earning a specified score. The FIDE website has the exact set of rules.

Chess Activities

The primary activity for chess players other than just playing games with family and friends, or a computer, or online, is tournament play. A tournament is where several to many players gather to play chess for a day or two, almost always on a weekend. Longer tournaments of three or four days often coincide with U.S. holidays, like Memorial Day. There's more on tournaments in Chapter 2, especially on the question most parents and coaches face: is my player ready for a tournament?

Simuls (Simultaneous exhibition)

Nothing is quite as awe-inspiring as watching one person play against 20, 30, 40, or more players at the same time. Sometimes tournament organizers contract with a Grandmaster or International Master to put on a simul. Often the simul occurs the Friday night before a two-day weekend tournament. There may be a small fee to play, but it is well worth it.

Just as sports fans know the players of their favorite sports, both past and present, chess players like to know this, too. In **Appendix B – Famous Players** are three lists of champions from the world of chess. To find out more about famous players, past and present, use your internet search engine.

Chapter 2 – Tournaments

Is my child ready for a tournament?

"How do I know whether my child is ready?"

Perhaps every parent, whether familiar with the world of chess tournaments, or not, asks this question.

The tournament environment is at once exciting and overwhelming to new players and parents. There appears to be some sort of order to everything, but it isn't all quite clear to the novice.

In this chapter we'll take a look at tournaments; how to know whether your child is ready, how to find them, and how they operate.

First, we'll look at the burning question about knowing if your child is ready, both in terms of skill and emotionally. The best way to prepare a player for a tournament is to work on the basic skills she should have, and make sure she has achieved those skills. Taking a player to a tournament without these basic and crucial skills would be like sending a batter to the plate without ever having seen a batting practice pitch.

Chess is a battle. It's a game, yes, but it requires so much from an individual who is pitted against another person. Both want to win the game, but the player who makes the strongest moves, and keeps his emotions in check, stands the best chance of winning. Chess is one mind against the other. A chess player is alone. He must rely on his memory and ability to think through a problem. There's no coach giving hints, like hold the bat up higher, and there's no cheer squad, *Saturday Night Live* skits notwithstanding.

Preparation is the key, and that's why we'll look at that list of basic skills now:

Basic skills

To ensure your child has a good first tournament experience, I recommend that you use the checklist on page 126. While all players, regardless of age or experience want to win every game played, it's an unrealistic expectation, especially for new players. The average player probably wins two or three games in a five-game tournament. Yes, of course, there are exceptions, but setting realistic expectations is important, particularly for young players. A good tournament experience, in my eyes, is one where the child had fun, learned something new, made new friends, *and* wants to do it again. It is not whether he won a game or "performed" well enough to place high in the standings. If your child did play well, and won several games, and placed high in the standings, then your child may have the makings of becoming a very good player.

However, it's been my experience, both personally and as a coach watching very good players on my team (and other teams), that today's tournament performance is not a guarantee that the next tournament will be the same. In some cases, yes, this is true, but even very good players have off-days, and don't play as well as usual–in baseball, this is called a hitting slump–and it happens for a variety of reasons, not the least of which is focus, or concentration, which can wane on "bad" days and affect play. Feeling ill has a direct negative effect on play and I recommend skipping a tournament if your child is ill. The other parents will thank you for not exposing their kids, and them, to a virus.

Here's the checklist of skills that I required my new players to have *before* they went to their first tournament. Some of them may seem obvious, but believe me, I've seen plenty of new players (from other schools) who didn't know some of this stuff and it cost them, either in games or emotions, or both.

Tournament Skills Checklist

☑	Demonstrated Skill or Knowledge
☐	Three parts of the game.
☐	Three parts of the opening.
☐	Opening moves for black and white, in response to both d4 and e4.
☐	Tactics – pins
☐	Tactics – forks
☐	Tactics – discovered attacks (check)
☐	Tactics – skewer
☐	Tactics – double attack
☐	Checkmate – Queen and Bishop
☐	Checkmate – Queen and Knight
☐	Checkmate – Queen and Rook
☐	Checkmate – Queen and King
☐	Checkmate – King and Rook
☐	Checkmate – King and Two Rooks
☐	Chess notation.
☐	Use a clock.

Once your child has shown you he has all of these skills, you're half-way to being ready for a tournament. Why half way? Emotions. Losing is hard on players of any sport, but in chess, losing carries a special kind of personal impact. Most kids play team sports where the *team* loses, and there can be some anonymity. True, there can be some spectacularly public individual errors, like dropping a fly ball or striking out, but if the team wins, those errors are forgotten. Like singles tennis, when a chess players loses a tournament game, his teammates, coach, parents, and the opposing player's teammates all know he lost. And no one else is responsible! He wasn't the pitcher throwing the game of his life only to lose because of another player's error. In chess you play your best and if you don't win, it's on you.

Sounds harsh doesn't it? I mean, come on, it's just a game after all, right? Yes, absolutely. The reality is that it's highly probable that your child will lose at least some games in her first tournament, but *there'll be many more games to play. Your daughter could win the next game or the next several.* She will learn something about the game and herself from a loss or even a string of losses.

Your job is to be able to provide the support your child needs after a loss. Remind her of the italicized comments above. Some kids can shake off a loss and are ready for the next game with no problems at all. Some players have trouble with losing and sometimes carry with them to the next game thoughts about what they did wrong in the previous game. Some kids are so upset they will cry. Some get angry at themselves and draw on that burning to play better. I've seen players lose a tough-fought game, buck up and beat the living daylights out of their next opponent. Some players were so good at this that they got a reputation and no one wanted to play them after a loss because it meant certain doom.

Your job is to know what will work best with your child. Comfort them or push them? That's not up to me–each child is different–but what I did was remind them of the italicized portion above, ask if they knew how the game became a lost game (note I don't ask, "do you know why you lost?" it's always "How did the game become lost?"). This allows them to disassociate themselves from the loss, even if it's ever so slightly, and look at the game objectively. Almost every time the reply was something like, yes, I hung a piece and missed it, or I moved such-and-such and got out of position.

You know your child best. You may have already seen how he handles losing, whether on a team sport, or perhaps just playing video games with his friends, or family.

Back to our original question: "How do I know whether my child is ready?" If she can demonstrate the skills and you're confident in her ability to withstand losing, she's ready.

One last thing: I've never heard of a child quitting chess because he couldn't stand losing.

Scholastic tournaments eligibility

Scholastic tournaments are open only to children in grades up to and including twelve, seniors in high school. Generally, they're open to K – 12, but very young players are sometimes also eligible.

Scholastic tournaments do not require a player to have qualified, in the sense of "advancing" to state or national. These tournaments are called "open" and any player who meets the requirements of being in K – 12 may play.

Some tournaments are invitational, and these do have qualifying criteria which may include the player's established rating (cannot be provisional), age, activity (number of tournament games), and residency.

The first tournament

If your child is playing in the chess club at school, the coach may have tournament information available. Be sure to ask the coach questions about tournament play. Here's a list of things you may want to ask, but always feel free to ask any question, no matter how unimportant it may seem. The coach is there to help your child have fun and play as well as he can.

Frequently Asked Questions about tournaments

1. Is my child ready to play?
   The coach can answer this question, but you can use my Tournament Skills Checklist found on page 126.
2. Will my child have to join USCF (United States Chess Federation)?
   Some scholastic tournaments do require USCF membership, and all Nationals and Supers (tournament types start on the next page) require it. USCF membership gives scholastic players the privilege of playing in USCF tournaments and getting a monthly magazine *Chess Life*

for Kids. Check out www.uschess.org for more information on the benefits of memberships.

3. Will my child play kids his own age, or play much older children?

> This depends on how the tournament is set up. Most large tournaments have sections by grade group, such as K – 3, 4 – 6, and so on. Others may have more grades in one group such as K – 8. You can find out how each tournament is set up by reading the tournament announcement (there's an example of one on page 131).

> Some tournaments are also divided into sections based on grade and rating, for example, 4 – 6 Under 1000, so be sure to find the correct and best section for your child.

4. Do tournaments give out awards?

> Almost all scholastic tournaments award medals and / or trophies. Often it's medals for individual players and trophies for teams.

5. How long do tournaments last?

> Most scholastic tournaments are one-day events, except for nationals, which may be three days. Plan on spending an entire day at a chess tournament as they will typically begin around 10:00 AM and play until 4:00 or 5:00 PM. Tournament announcements must give the times of all rounds, and if you look at the time for the last round, then add the amount of time required for each round, you'll know about when the last round will finish. Be sure to multiply the time for each round by two. For example, if the announcement says it's G30, this means 30 minutes each player, so 60 minutes total for the game, maximum.

Types of scholastic tournaments

School sponsored

A school sponsored tournament is one that usually takes place in a school building, often in the student cafeteria which will have enough seating and tables for all players. Many states have a calendar just for scholastic tournaments.

State

Most states have a tournament toward the end of the school year called the State Championship, although some are early in the school year. Typically, the tournament will have sections for elementary, middle and high school. Some states may combine elementary and middle and call it K – 8.

Nationals

The United States Chess Federation helps sponsor an annual national level tournament where players from all over the U.S.A. come to compete. These tournaments are broken down into elementary, middle and high school.

Supernationals

Every four years, the national tournament for each level, elementary, middle, and high school are held at the same location. The first of these "Super" tournaments was held in Knoxville, TN. In 1997, I was privileged to take a team of four players, including my son, to this tournament. It's quite a wonderful sight, over 4,000 student players filling a hall, playing chess . . . in total silence! My son played in one more Super in 2001 held in Kansas City, MO. And again there were more than 4,000 players. Two Grandmasters (GM) were there putting on instruction sessions, and we even got to meet International Master (IM) Josh Waitzkin, of *Searching for Bobby Fischer* fame. Bruce Pandolfini, Josh's coach, well-known before working with Josh, was there, too. We took a lot of pictures and obtained Waitzkin's and Pandolfini's autographs on one of our vinyl tournament boards.

Finding Scholastic tournaments

If your child's school has a chess club and coach, or if you have a personal coach, he should have information about upcoming tournaments. If neither of these is true, you can search the internet for your state's chess association and should be able to find either links to scholastic information, or a contact name.

Another place is to buy a copy of USCF's *Chess Life* at a local bookstore. It has a Tournament Life section toward the back that lists tournaments by state. Here's an example of what a tournament announcement looks like:

Mar 27, 2010
Prairie Chess Series Tournament #2 (USCF Rated)

Four sections; K-2, 3-5, 6-8, and 9-12. Sections will be combined if less than 5 players in grade range. 4 Games – 30 minutes per player per game. All Players play 4 games. **Where:** Prairie Creek Intermediate Cafeteria ,Prairie Creek Intermediate School ,401 76th Avenue ,Cedar Rapids ,IA 52404 **Reg:** On-site from 9:00 am to 10:00 am. **Rounds:** Rounds: 1 at 10:30, 2 at Noon, Rounds 3 and 4 ASAP. **Entry Fee:** $10 if registered before tournament, $15 on site. $25 for all three tournaments if registered in advance (by email okay, pay on site). **Prize Info:** Tournament Awards: Trophies 1st through 3rd Medals for 4th through 6th. Series Awards: 1st through 3rd. Highest individual total score from all three events. Highest school total score (all players) from all 3 events. **US Chess Federation (USCF) membership required.** On-Site Available. **Send Entry Fee to:** James Hodina 3411 Blue Pt. Ct. SW Cedar Rapids, Iowa 52404 319-390-6525 or james.hodina@mchsi.com. **Additional Info:** James Hodina, james.hodina@mchsi.com, www.chessiniowa.org. Endnote [1]

How to read this thing: first, the date and name of tournament. Then it says this tournament is divided into four sections by grade, followed by the game time (30 minutes per player – sometimes noted as G30). Next is where, and it tells you when registration is and the time. It gives you the entry fee, offering a lower price for early registration (by mail). The prizes are listed, and whether USCF membership is required. The last is where to send registration.

Once you've located a tournament and have registered, or plan to register on-site, you're ready to go. Here are some tips to making a tournament day fun and eventful:

- Make sure your child gets plenty of rest the night before.
- Some tournament locations have a concessions stand where you can buy lunches – find out before you go.
- Determine *before* the day of tournament whether you are going to eat out for breakfast and lunch, and possibly dinner. If you decide to eat out, use the internet to find

eating places close to the tournament that meet your budget and dietary needs.

- If you plan to take all meals, prepare them the night before.
- Take healthy snacks (sugary foods may have a detrimental effect on your player, especially early on) and drinks.
- If you have a tournament board and set, take it with you. Make sure the board has your or your child's name on it, and put initials on the bottom of each piece.
- Most tournaments provide score sheets, but you can buy a scorebook from www.uschess.org.
- Take several pencils.
- Take something for your child to do between rounds, a book to read, for example.
- Take something for *you* to do. Parents often visit with each other during and between rounds, but you might need some private time. Your stress level is going to be elevated, believe me.
- Take a bottle of pain reliever like Tylenol, some for you and some for your child, just in case.
- Take some band-aids and antiseptic ointment. Don't ask how I learned this one.
- Take any medicines you or your child would normally take during the daytime.
- And lastly – take a camera!

How tournaments work

Who plays? Most tournaments use the Swiss pairings method, which is designed so that *all* registered players can play *all* rounds. It is not lose and go home. Registration is usually between 8:30 and 9:30 am. There is an entry fee that varies by tournament. This fee covers the expense of the medals and trophies, and the United States Chess Federation rating fee. Most scholastic tournaments consist of four to six rounds, or games. Round one begins about 9:30 or 10:00 am. The time for each game available is in the tournament announcement.

A lunch break is sometimes provided, but when it is not, players eat between games. Depending on where the tournament is, at a school, a hotel meeting room, there may be a concessions stand where everyone can purchase lunch.

The last round is usually finished by 4:30 or 5:00 pm and scholastic tournaments typically have a nice award ceremony right after the results are finalized.

Tournament Pairings

The assignment of opponents (pairings) is an interesting, but complex process. Most tournament directors use a computer program to make the pairings, and as mentioned earlier, use the Swiss System, which is the most commonly used pairing method in the United States. Using a computer program saves time and provides clarity, especially for tie-breaks.

Here's how it works for the first round:
1. the computer ranks all players in descending order according to their rating, with first-time players ("unrated") being assigned to the bottom. Unrated has nothing to do with skill. Woe to the player who assumes an unrated player is going to be an easy win. All players who do not have a rating have this designation.
2. the computer divides the group into two halves, a top and a bottom.
3. then it pairs the top player in each group together; so for example, if there are 100 players, the number 1 player is paired with the number 51 player, number 2 plays number 52, and so on. Example:

1	⇔	51
2	⇔	52

The player's color is assigned for every game by the computer program that manages the pairings. Generally speaking, a player will alternate colors, but due to the rules of pairings, if two paired players are both "due" a certain color, one will get the opposite instead, so it is possible to have one color twice in a row. The pairings program tries to find a way for a player never to have black three times in a row.

All subsequent rounds are paired based upon players who have like, or similar, scores, called a score group. For example, after round one there are three possibilities a player can have:

1. 1 point for a win
2. ½ point for a draw (tie)
3. 0 (zero) points for a loss

The computer groups all 1 pointers together, all ½ pointers together and all zero pointers together. It ranks and pairs players within those groups again using the same process as described earlier for the first round. Sometimes, there is an odd number of players in one or more of the score groups. When this happens the computer will move players up or down a score group (say from being in the ½ point group to the 1 point group) to be able to pair the highest scores first.

Its purpose is to try and provide a clear winner after six rounds, because as the tournament progresses, players with winning scores rise to the top, and by the final round, players with the highest scores will be paired together. Depending on the number of players, there may be a clear winner after all rounds are completed. For example, in a typical tournament there might be six rounds. If at the end of those rounds, there is only one player with a perfect score of 6 – 0, then she is declared the winner. If there are two or more players with a perfect score (if the tournament is large, players can't possibly play everyone), the winner is determined by tie breaks. There are many ways to calculate a tie-break score, but the most common one that is used first is for the computer to add together the total points scored by the opponents who faced each of the players involved in the tie.

If your child is playing as a member of a team, when individuals score points, the team also scores points based upon the top four or five scores. This adds to the excitement for the players, as they watch the team scoreboard during the tournament.

Teammates do not play each other in scholastic tournaments. If your child and siblings are playing in a tournament that is non-scholastic tournament, you can request (of the tournament director) that they do not play each other. If the tournament is large enough, most directors will be happy to accommodate you.

That's enough on the mechanics of pairings. For more information you can always read the *Official Rules of Chess*. Be sure to always get the latest edition. You can find out which one that is by going to the USCF web site: www.uschess.org.

The tournament paperwork

The tournament director uses computer reports to keep track of everything going on in the tournament and to provide information for players, coaches and parents. These reports are:
- Pairings sheet
- Individual wall chart, or standings
- Team wall chart, or standings
- Cross tables

In the next few sections, you'll learn how to read these reports.

How to read the Pairings sheet

The Pairings sheet tells each player which board number he will be playing on for that round, which color he has, and his opponent's name and rating, and their score so far. In the sample Pairings sheet on the next page we find this information:
- date. 6/8/10
- Tournament name. Sample Elementary School K – 5
- Round number. 1
- The board numbers and names for six players. Player A and B are on board 1. Board numbers are placed by each board in the tournament room. Board 1 will have the highest ranked player in round one.
- The ratings for each player. Player, A is 1462, and Player, F is UNR (unrated).
- Their score so far, which in the first round, are all zero.

6/8/10 Sample Elementary School K – 5, round 1
Pairing sheet, Page 1

Board	White	Black
1	____ Player, A 1462 (0.0)	____ Player, B 982 (0.0)
2	____ Player, C 1302 (0.0)	____ Player, D 950 (0.0)
3	____ Player, E 1283 (0.0)	____ Player, F UNR (0.0)

This is where your player will record his score, which will be one of these possibilities:

- 1 point for a win
- ½ point for a draw (tie)
- 0 (zero) points for a loss

Here's what a Pairings sheet could look like after the players have written in their scores.

6/8/10 Sample Elementary School K – 8, round 1
Pairing sheet, Page 1

Board	White	Black
1	_1_ Player, A 1462 (0.0)	_0_ Player, B 982 (0.0)
2	_1_ Player, C 1302 (0.0)	_0_ Player, D 950 (0.0)
3	_0_ Player, E 1283 (0.0)	_1_ Player, F UNR (0.0)

The Pairing sheet for round 4 might look like this. I've added some different players. Note the scores for each player.
Remember, the computer tries to pair players with the same score.

6/8/10 Sample Elementary School K – 8, round 4
Pairing sheet, Page 1

Board	White	Black
1	____ Player, K 1250 (3.0)	____ Player, A 1462 (3.0)
2	____ Player, C 1302 (2.5)	____ Player, D 950 (2.5)
3	____ Player, F UNR (2.0)	____ Player, M 745 (2.0)

Not shown in the previous examples is each player's eight-digit USCF ID. This will be present only if the tournament is USCF rated.

Getting your player to the right place.

When your player is new to tournaments, you should help him find his name on the Pairings sheet. I recommend that you have him write the board number, and his opponent's name and rating on the score sheet while standing at the Pairings Sheet.

Help him find the board (all the boards will have a number card, or card-tent to identify it). When his opponent arrives, he should always ask for the opponent's name, and check it against what he wrote down from the Pairings Sheet. It's not uncommon for players to go to the wrong board and this helps prevent seating errors.

Once you are satisfied your player is in the right place, wish him luck, and if you're so inclined, say it to his opponent, too. Then leave. Go at least far enough away that your player can't see you, there may be exceptions, your child may want you to be in view at least until the game starts.

Byes

A "Bye" occurs under two circumstances:
1. there is an odd number of players, so one person has no opponent. A half-point is awarded for a bye. In some tournaments, non-scholastic, the director may have a "house" player (or the director himself) who will play only when someone would have received a bye. The Pairing sheet will have "BYE" in place of the opponent's name.
2. a player may need to miss a round for personal reasons. In order to receive the half-point for the Bye, the player (or parent / coach) must tell the director before the pairings are being prepared for the round to be missed. My advice: tell the director as soon as you

know your player will miss a round, the earlier the better. Your player will receive the half-point.

Withdrawing from a tournament

To withdraw from a tournament means that your player will be not be playing any more games for the remainder of the tournament. If your player cannot finish the tournament, perhaps he became ill, or the family has plans, the courteous thing to do is to withdraw him from the tournament. You must advise the director your player is withdrawing, otherwise, he will pair your player for a round, but your player's opponent will sit down with an empty chair across from him. On the standings, the games will appear as "U" or something similar to indicate un-played. He will NOT receive any half-points for the un-played games.

What happens when my player sits down across from his opponent?

When two players sit down on opposite sides of the board, there are a few things that occur. Some are almost on the subconscious level.

1. They size each other up. Physical attributes and demeanor are all processed by the part of the brain that does a threat analysis. Experienced scholastic players are not intimidated by physically bigger opponents (see the section titled David vs. Goliath). I've watched plenty of "big" boys lose games to smaller boys and girls. Psychologically speaking, you might say that the bigger opponent (or older if you prefer) sized up the eventual winner as a non-threat, only to discover on the board (too late, I might add), that he was wrong.
2. They set up the board if it's not already. Often the board is already set up from a previous round, and in this case they may need to turn the board around so each has the correct color.
3. Exchange names and rating, and sometimes also the name of their school.

4. They each write down (or verify) the information on the score sheet and include the round number.
5. They wait for the announcement to start the clock.
6. If they don't know each other, they may chat to pass the time and maybe settle their nerves.
7. If they do know each other and have become friends, they will certainly chat, but once the game begins it's all business; play hard, play to win.
8. If they know each other but perhaps have developed what I'll call a non-friendly relationship (for many reasons, but maybe they just don't like each other), they may look around the tournament room, at the board, at their hands, anywhere but at their opponent.
9. When the "start your clocks" announcement is given, the players should shake hands and give a friendly "Good luck" to their opponent.
10. The player playing black hits the clock button or lever that starts white's clock and the game is on.

The end of the game

Just a few pages earlier we talked about the three possible outcomes of the game:
- Win
- Loss
- Draw

When the game is over, regardless of the outcome, the players should shake hands and say, "good game" or "nice game," as a show of respect and courtesy for their opponent.

When the game ends in checkmate, sometimes one player will look surprised (not necessarily the losing player) and say, "I think that's checkmate." The game is over when *both* players agree that it is checkmate. Teach your player to know checkmate, and when in doubt, call for a tournament director. Never argue with your opponent, just call for help.

Draws require certain procedures. A player should only offer a draw when it *his* turn to move, not his opponent's. For more information on draws, see Chapter 8 – A short rules list for tournament players.

After the round is complete, the players must enter their scores because *both* players are responsible whether they won, lost or drew. As a coach, I stressed this point every season. Sometimes mistakes happen and a player will enter the score incorrectly. If the other player doesn't check it, the tournament director has no idea that the score is wrong. An example would be a player who won not putting a "1" by his name, only to discover later, and too late, that he didn't get the point he'd earned.

How to read the Wall chart (Standings sheet)

The wall chart shows information about all players and what place they are in after the specified round. Rankings are based on total score (points earned). If several players are tied in points, then the computer ranks them based on several tie-breaks. The rankings are then based on a specified order of the tie-breaks. Here is a sample wall chart.

Sample Elementary School K – 8
Placement by Score/Ties – Round 6

Pair	Place	Name	School	Gr	Rtg	Scr	Tie 1
2	1	Nathan	WATM	8	1191	5.5	24.0
11	2	Jeffrey	LSAW	8	921	5.5	21.5
7	3	William	ARAM	6	1433	5.0	21.0

In the above sample we see that Nathan won first place based on a tie-break. He and Jeffrey both scored 5.5, but Nathan's tie-break is 24.0 compared to Jeffrey's 21.5. As mentioned before, the computer will likely use several tie-breaks (perhaps six). The first tie-break is almost always the accumulated score of the player's opponents. In Nathan's case, his opponents (six of them) scored 24.0 points all together. Jeffrey's opponents scored 21.5. For more details on tie-breaks, read the *Official Rules of Chess*.

If there are teams, then there will also be a wall chart for teams, and it will be similar to the previous sample.

How to read the Cross table

A cross table shows information about each player, round by round. Their opponents are identified by the place number in which they finished. This example shows that Nathan played players who finished 9th, 10th, 3rd, 8th, 12th, and 2nd. He won all his games except for the game against 12, which was a draw.

Sample Elementary School K – 8 cross table
6/8/10

No	Name	School	Rtg	Scr	Rd1	Rd2	Rd3	Rd4	Rd5	Rd6
1	Nathan	WATM	1191	5.5	W9	W10	W3	W8	D12	W2
2	Jeffrey	LSAW	921	5.5	W29	W15	D4	W2	W6	W7
3	William	ARAM	1433	5.0	W33	W18	L1	W4	W8	W9

Sportsmanship and tournament rules

Sportsmanship is extremely important in chess and there are strict rules of behavior. Chess demands that both players play to win using their own minds and the skills they've learned. This means that in most games there will be a winner and a loser (some games are draws, a tie). Chess teaches players to win *and* lose graciously.

Winning and losing are a part of the learning process. All players lose games, even World Champions. Much can be learned from the games that are lost. Experienced players first study the games they *lost*, then they look over the ones they won. There's more on sportsmanship near the end of this chapter in the section called Spôrts'mən-shǐp (noun).

No coaching allowed during games!

Coaches, parents, and other players who are watching a game are forbidden to give advice or in any way communicate information to the players. Failure to abide by this rule can result in the loss of a point for the player who breaks the rule, the player playing the game, and the team would lose a point.

Here's a list of information I always provided to new players and their parents. Feel free to copy the two pages.

Players' Tournament Rules and Advice

- You are here for the fun of it!
- Always do your best.
- When the director says to begin your game, be sure to shake your opponent's hand and wish him good luck.
- You don't have to call check. Your opponent should be able to see it.
- If your opponent makes an illegal move, such as not noticing he's in check, tell him before you make your next move.
- Any time you have a question, stop the clock (if you have one), raise your hand and wait for a coach or director to help you.
- If someone around you is bothering you such as talking or making noises like pencil tapping or other annoying things, raise your hand. DO NOT speak to the person yourself.
- If you touch a piece and can legally move it, you *must* move it. If you touch your opponent's piece and can legally capture it, you *must* capture it.
- If you are recording your moves (required for 30 minute or longer games) when *either* you or your opponent has 5 minutes left, you may stop recording. You can ask a teammate or friend to record the rest of the game for you.
- You are free to get up from your game if you need to go to the restroom, get a drink of water or just to stretch and clear your mind. Just be aware that your clock may start running while you are gone.
- If you are playing with a clock, and you do leave your game, wait until it is your opponent's turn to move. Be sure to start your opponent's clock before leaving the board.
- You must know the board position before you leave, so you can mentally compare it when you return to find out what piece your opponent moved and to make sure it is correct. Your opponent is not required to tell you what

piece was moved, although he might out of common courtesy.

- After your game is over, you must record the result of the game on the score sheet, usually hanging on the wall near the tournament director.
- If you are watching other players' games, do not talk to either player.
- If a player's flag falls while you are watching the game, DO NOT say anything! One of the players involved in the game must notice it.
- If you want to talk to someone else also watching a game, walk away from the game first.
- Do not stand close to the table when watching other games.
- Go over your game with a teammate or coach. There are two reasons for this: 1) it helps you find any errors in the score sheet, and 2) by going over the game you can find your strong and weak moves. This will improve your understanding of the game and help you become a stronger player.
- When the last round is over and all results are finalized, the awards ceremony will begin.

David vs. Goliath

One of the beautiful things about chess is that physical attributes and age don't matter, knowledge does. As I mentioned earlier, I've seen "big" or older kids defeated by smaller or younger opponents. A story that comes to mind is when I was coaching a team from a small rural town. We traveled to a tournament in Kansas City, KS. At that time, scholastic tournaments were run as grades K-12. My youngest player, a second grader, was playing in his second tournament. He was a little guy, but he knew how to play solid chess. In one of the earlier rounds, he was paired against a big red-headed boy, a junior who was four times bigger and nine years older. I spoke to my player briefly as he seemed intimidated by this big boy. I simply said to play his game and forget who he's playing. I watched them set up from a distance, and noted the expression on the junior's face; the message was clear: easy pickings.

The game started and I wandered away to check on my other players. About fifteen minutes later, I went back to check on the David vs. Goliath game, and was not surprised at all to see that the game was even in material and my player had a strong position. He was indeed playing his game. I checked the older boy's expression and it was now one of disbelief, that he'd have to fight hard to win. Which he did, eventually, with the game going into a long end game. I was so proud of my player. He went on to become one of the top players on our team over the years and he was never intimidated by bigger kids again.

Is it checkmate?

As we discussed in Lesson 10, your player must know what is and isn't checkmate. It's heartbreaking to walk by a game and hear a player say triumphantly, "Checkmate," but when you look at the board, it's not checkmate at all. Since we're not allowed to interfere with a game, the "losing" player usually just shakes hands and walks away dejectedly. Make sure your player(s) know what checkmate is, and if in doubt, they have the right to call for the tournament director and ask. The director will only answer "yes" or "no" and will not explain why it's not checkmate, but then at least your player knows he should keep on looking.

The first tournament win

The first time your child wins a tournament game, be prepared for it. The vast majority of kids will come running to you or the coach with a wide, beaming grin. The outcome of the game is obvious. A tournament win is an enormous boost to a child's confidence. Suddenly, she realizes that everything she's learned, and that all the things said by you or the coach, are true. Your reaction to the win must reinforce those thoughts. Give your child lots of smiles and pats, and high-fives. Let her tell the rest of the team (if you're with a team), and they should be taught to congratulate each player who wins a game.

Be certain she wrote her score on the pairings sheet – go with her to see it, and confirm it is correct. It would be demoralizing to lose that hard-earned point and then be paired incorrectly in the next round because the score wasn't posted correctly or at all. Some tournament directors will come track down a player with no result written, but they are not obligated to do so. And if her opponent wrote down the results, what if he made a mistake, or worse, purposely altered the result? You must avoid these situations. Each player is responsible for making sure the score was recorded correctly, but you as the parent or coach must help them.

If there's time before the next round, have your player go over the game. See if she can pinpoint the move or move sequence that led to her win. Let her shine!

Just before the next round's pairings are posted, take a moment to congratulate your player once again, then be sure to remind her to stayed focused on the next game, and to play strong!

The first tournament loss

If your child is a pretty strong player, odds are fair that his first *win* could happen in round one of his first tournament. No matter when the win happens, there's bound to be a *loss* coming. So how to handle the first one? I typically asked my players coming back to the team table with a dejected look on their face this question about their loss: "Did you play your best?" New players will usually reply yes, but may not know exactly why they lost. Experienced players often will say, yes, but on move 27, I [pick one: left a piece hanging, missed mate, went down in the exchange]. They understand when the game went from a possible win to an outright loss.

The first loss may or may not be a big deal for your child. It's best to react in accordance with their reaction, but always hide any personal disappointment you may feel. If they are nonchalant about it, they may already understand that you win some, you lose some, and there's always another game. What you have to watch out for is defeatism. If they say things like, "I'll never win a game," or "Everyone is better than I am," get yourself ready. You have to squelch that train of thought before it leaves the station. If you don't, it'll continue building steam, and each time he loses, that belief gets reinforced and it becomes, "See, I told you so."

It's very important to go over a game they lost. They must learn where the other player won it. Was it a blunder? Or as above: left a piece hanging, missed mate, went down in the exchange? Once you identify where the loss started, you can work on the ideas of how to avoid that in the future. Remind your player that all good chess players say the same thing about losses: that they learn more from a loss than a win.

Just before the next round's pairings are posted, be sure to encourage your child to play strong and make strong moves! You'll be surprised how much this can help a child.

The perfect tournament

If your child has become a strong tournament player, and is winning 80% (about) of his games on a regular bases, odds are increasing in his favor that he might have a perfect day, a tournament with all wins. In our Kansas scholastic tournaments, we played six games per tournament, and so our first perfect day occurred when my oldest players were in the sixth grade. My son Nathan was winning game after game, and by the end of the fifth round we knew he could have a perfect day. In round six, because of the way pairings are designed, to get players with the same score to "rise," Nathan was playing another kid who had won five games. It was a tough game, as you'd expect, but Nathan made all the best moves and won. This also meant he won the tournament, since he was the only perfect 6-0. That was the capstone to our team's sixth straight first-place finish. That was a happy day, and one I still cherish.

Playing a higher rated player or Kids playing adults

Pairings, especially in the first round, often pit players of very unequal strength (as measured by their ratings) so one player is playing "up," or against a higher rated player. In terms of statistics, if the rating difference is 400 points or more, the lower rated player has a tremendously diminished "chance" of winning. However, I have witnessed many, many "upsets" where the lower rated player beat the higher rated player.

Whether your child's opponent has a higher rating, or is an adult, the question is: how do you prepare your child for a game with such an imbalance? Remind her that her opponent is human, is subject to making mistakes, and that she must play strong and think solidly.

Non-scholastic tournaments, USCF

Some scholastic organizations and schools are not affiliated with the USCF. This is oftentimes a financial consideration. These tournaments adhere to the same set of rules, and are played in the same format as USCF rated tournaments. Many provide a rating of their own. You may have the choice of having your player(s) play in some USCF and some non-USCF tournaments. My recommendation is to have your child play as often as possible regardless of the tournament's status.

Spôrts'mən-shĭp (noun):

Conduct and attitude considered as befitting participants in sports, especially fair play, courtesy, striving spirit, and grace in losing.

"Be a good sport." "Shake their hand." "Tell them 'good game'." "You don't want to be a sore loser, do you?"

All kids who play sports hear these comments from parents, coaches, or other players. And sometimes other things are said; hurtful, berating, demeaning comments that destroy a child's self esteem and confidence.

Notice that the definition of sportsmanship does not include the word "win."

In the world of chess, sportsmanship is the expected norm. The rest of this chapter is on this topic.

Integrity

All major sports have one or more umpires (or referees) to watch the players and make decisions (calls) that directly affect the game. Some sports have even employed the use of instant replay to help the referees make the right call. The players themselves do not make calls, or influence the decision made by the referee. Yes, I know the argument that when a player shows his disagreement with a call, perhaps the next time the umpire will make a call that benefits that player's team, a make-up call. But the truth is, the umpires represent the rule book, and make calls for infractions of the rules (a personal foul, perhaps), or determine whether a pitch is a strike or ball, or whether the wide receiver was inbounds and the catch is good.

To my knowledge, golf is the only major sport where the players umpire themselves. They assess penalty strokes on themselves for various infractions, most of which probably went unnoticed by the other players, the tournament marshals, and even the viewing audience, whether live or watching on television.

Sometimes, though, it is another person who notices an infraction by a player and tells a marshal. A quite famous example of this happened some years ago to a well-known golfer of the time. This player had driven his tee shot left off the fairway and under a pine tree. The branches were too low for him to stand erect and make a swing, so instead, he got down on both knees and made a great little shot that got him out of the trouble. He was leading the tournament at the time (Saturday play) and went on to finish the day still ahead. That evening, a viewer called in to report that the player had broken a rule and must take a penalty of two strokes. The infraction that went unnoticed by almost everyone? The player had laid a golf towel on the ground (the ground was damp) to protect his trousers, and had placed his knees on the towel. By rule, this was "assistance" and was forbidden. The two stroke penalty cost him the tournament. An obscure rule, to be sure, but still a rule.

Chess is completely different. The rules state in so many words that only the players may make a call that a rule has been broken. The most common call is that an opponent has made an illegal move, such as moving into check.

The closest approximation to the umpire is the tournament director. So in our example above, the player who calls for the tournament director will have first stopped the clock. When the tournament director arrives, both players plead their case and the tournament director makes a binding decision. Sometimes, he may ask players near the board where the question arose if they saw what happened. He will make every effort to be fair. Once he makes his decision, it is final.

What is different here is that the players themselves called the rule infraction. It is only when players disagree on what happened that a tournament director is called to the board. To further show the difference between chess and other "refereed" sports let's take a look at what would happen if the tournament director was watching a game where a player just made an illegal move. What do you think the tournament director would do?

1. Would he stop the game and tell the player making the illegal move to take it back and make a legal move?
2. Would he do nothing?

The rules are quite clear: It depends! This is the one exception to having a player "request" help from a director. By the rules of chess, the tournament director could do nothing, and only act as a witness if asked by a player, or he could correct the move. Directors will have made a decision prior to the tournament as to which position they will take. In most scholastic tournaments, the director would do nothing.

Not being able to advise a player during a game is why coaching chess is sometimes very hard on the coach. Unlike youth baseball where the coach is making decisions all the time, in chess, a coach, tournament director, parent, teammate, or other spectator, cannot interfere with a game in progress.

Let's look at some other examples of where you as the parent or coach might be tempted to point out something to your player.

Your player is involved in a game where the clock is running out for one or both of the players. There is typically a crowd around games that run down to the wire and you can see everyone trying to jockey into position to see the clock. Both players know the situation and frequently glance at the clock, one hoping to see his opponent's flag fall (or if a digital clock, run to zero), or hoping that he can checkmate his opponent before his own clock runs out. In either case, both players are sweating. You're watching this game and a clock runs out. It's your player's opponent! Your player has won on time. Fantastic! But wait. Neither player has noticed the clock. The player whose clock has run out makes his move, and hits his clock. Now your player is on the clock. How could they not notice? you wonder. Oh my, what do you do? Should you yell out, "Flag!"?

No. Absolutely not. This is interference. And the penalty? If you or one of your player's teammates calls out, "Flag!" your player forfeits the game. Harsh? Yes, but that's the rule.

When a game is down to the final moments, a tournament director is bound to be present, just for the above possibility, he wants to be there to see for himself what happens. Then he will not have to rely on "testimony" by others. This is generally how the forfeiture penalty would be assessed.

Sometimes a player will inadvertently touch one piece while trying to grab another to move; when this happens some players will cry out, "Touch move!" And try to force the moving player to move the first piece touched. This is when the experienced player knows he needs to call for a tournament director.

The final word: don't "help" your player(s) in any way.

Over parenting - Parents' behavior - not always parental

Along with the idea of integrity, and the above admonition to not help your player, here's further commentary on parental behavior in the tournament setting. As with any sport, watching someone you love make a mistake in a chess game is difficult. It's very difficult. You may inwardly groan at a weak move or a blunder, but you should not under any circumstances do it out loud. There are two reason for this: first, if your child hears you, you have just told him you disapprove of his move, and as kids sometimes do, he will extrapolate that to mean you disapprove of him. It's not my place or intent to teach you about parenting your child, but there is truth to that statement for *some* kids, so be aware. The second reason is that if you groan out loud, you might alert your child's opponent to the blunder. Sometimes, especially in games between relatively inexperienced players, one player will blunder, but the opponent *will not realize* it and will make a move that doesn't capitalize on the error.

At many tournaments, depending on where it is in the United States, parents and coaches are permitted to roam the game room to observe the games. Oftentimes, the coaches act as assistant tournament directors in that they can answer questions by players (not from their own team, though) when a player has "called" for a tournament director. For your benefit, here's a list of how parents and coaches, and teammates, are expected to behave in the tournament room:

- Never speak to players during play.
- Never touch a piece or the board.
- If you are watching one of your player's games, stand to the side of the board, or better yet, behind *your* player.

- Do not make eye contact with your player, or smile, or gesture, or cough, or clear your throat, even a hand wave "Hello," it could be misconstrued as "help." If in doubt, don't do it.
- Do not say anything if you see a breach of rules.

In my years of experience coaching kids at tournaments, I can say I only once witnessed a parent helping her child during the game. The parent was a first-time chess parent, and to give her the benefit of the doubt, I'll say she wasn't aware of the expected tournament behavior. Here's what we found her doing in the first round: she sat in chair a few feet from her son's board, facing him. He was probably in the third or fourth grade. When it was his move, he would hover his hand over a piece and look at mom. She would nod or shake her head. Really, this happened. As soon as we saw this, we called the tournament director and he quietly called her away and explained that she could not help her child.

There are stories, some undoubtedly true, in various parts of the United Sates, where parents and coaches have been accused of helping their player(s) by hand signals, much like a third base coach in baseball, a tug of the ear for Rook, a nose touch for a Knight, and so forth. This caused many scholastic tournament directors to forbid coaches and parents, and players who have finished their games, to be in the game room. Period.

Chapter 3 – Players getting stronger

How do I know if my player is getting stronger? What do I watch for? These are good questions and there are a few answers to help you determine where your player "fits" in the world of competitive chess.

First, is your player's chess rating. As we discussed in Chapter 1, a player earns a rating based on his performance against other rated players. This is the advantage of playing in USCF rated tournaments, which most, but not all scholastic tournaments are. In our case, in the state of Kansas, at the time my son and his teammates were playing, the Kansas Scholastic Chess Association tournaments were not USCF rated. So the KSCA used it's own rating system which was based on the same formula as the USCF.

Regardless of the overall playing strength of the players in your area, your player's rating will always be a relative strength to the field. For example, let's say the average rating in your scholastic tournaments is 1200. If your child is higher than the average, then he is likely winning more games than he's losing, and vice-versa.

Intermediate skill players

An intermediate scholastic player's rating could fall in the range of 1200 – 1400, or so – this is not science. Irrespective of ratings, an intermediate skill player is going to be able to play relatively sound games, with few outright blunders. Notice I didn't say no blunders. All players, at all levels, make blunders, some are more devastating than others, but the blunders still occur.

Here's a list of things an intermediate player will have in his chess toolbox:

1. Checkmate patterns involving the Queen, Rooks, Knights and Bishops in combination with each other.
2. King and Queen checkmate.
3. King and Rook checkmate.
4. King and pawn (promotion), then King and Queen checkmate.
5. Pins, skewers, and forks.
6. Understands the principles of the opening.
7. Knows a solid opening for white, and can play a sound opening for black against both e4 and d4 openings.
8. Understands the idea of winning the exchange, and knows what to do after getting up in material.

Upping the challenges

Once a player has displayed the knowledge noted above for an intermediate player, it's time to up the challenges to his play and thinking. There are several ways to go about this. However, it will require study time, just as does a subject in school. How much time? Well, I don't know, but perhaps you can start with an hour a week. I do suggest finding out whether your child really does want to do the work. Once you've done that, then you can make plans for the study times. Here's a list of topics to begin working on. These are not in any order, and just represent items to choose from. I found it best to focus on one item for a time, maybe a few weeks, then switch to another to help keep your child interested and reduce the likelihood of boredom.

1. Have your child begin playing a good computer program. There are several on the market. I use Chessmaster and it works very well as an opponent because you can select "personalities" who play at known ratings.
    a. If your child has a rating, have him begin play against the computer at a level roughly equal to his own.
    b. I recommend a game time of 30 minutes.
    c. Have the computer run an analysis of the game and print it.
    d. Go over it together.
    e. Start him on games against higher rated computer opponents.
2. Study the endgame. As players advance in skill, and if they have a rating, it will be going up, checkmates during the middle game become more difficult and occur less often. This means more games last into a true end game. The player who realizes the game will progress to an end game, and understands which positions create an advantage for him, will win more games. There are many, many books on the end game, and the hardest part will be selecting one.
3. Study tactics. Especially focus on ideas surrounding winning material and sacrifices. Josh Waitzkin's book *Attacking Chess* is a great place to start.
4. Increase knowledge of openings. As players face stronger opponents who will typically have more than one or two openings under their belt, it's important to know how to play against the opening. A knowledge of opening traps is a good thing to study, especially gambits (a free pawn, generally) will show your player what to do, and maybe more importantly, what not to do.

Advanced and exceptional players

An advanced scholastic player's rating might fall into the range of about 1400 – 1600, and an exceptional player will be above 1600. Again, these are suggestions, and are not set in stone. Depending on your location, and the overall strength of the scholastic tournament players in your area, your child's relative strength is a key indicator. In other words, if your child's rating is 1400, and the average rating is also 1400, then your child may be closer to an intermediate player. On the other hand, if the reverse its true, and your child's rating is 1600 and the average rating is 1400, then your child might be an advanced player. If you have a chess club coach, feel free to discuss your child's skill set, strengths, and weaknesses to determine what you should do.

Intermediate and advanced players as teachers

I was, and currently am, fortunate to have several players who play solid chess and are also able and willing to teach. If you have players who are playing well above the rest of the club, you should consider asking them if they'd be interested in helping with the other players, especially new players. You'd be surprised how well this works. I recently did exactly this (a ninth grader working with a fifth grader), then asked the more experienced player how the new player did. His response was that the younger player surprised him and had a good solid grasp of the game. What a wonderful thing to hear.

This has benefits for the experienced player, too. Many times, while teaching another person, the teacher is required to explain in a way that helps his own understanding of the subject. This then deepens a teacher's knowledge, always a positive.

How to know when you yourself can't help your child anymore

If the items I mentioned above are unclear to you, or you believe you don't have the knowledge yourself, or when you play your child, he beats you regularly (my son starting beating me when he was 13), it may be time to consider hiring a chess coach.

Finding a personal chess coach

Before embarking on the search for a personal coach, I again stress that you determine whether your child will be willing to take on the challenges of the extra work load a coach will demand.

There are several ways to find a chess coach for your child. Some coaching services exist online and they provide very good instruction, and it is one-on-one coaching. My personal preference is that a coach is face-to-face with the student. One way to find a coach is to search online for chess coaches and examine the first three or four results. Most sites (or online chess schools) provide testimonials, read them.

If you have chess contacts, such as your child's school's coach, or if you know someone involved in running tournaments, or is involved with your state's chess association, ask them for recommendations. These folks can also assist you in your search for a face-to-face coach.

If you don't have any contacts for help, try an internet search for "your state" plus "Chess Association." This should take you to the web site for your state's governing organization for chess. Examine the links, look for someone called the "Scholastic Coordinator" or something similar. His email may be present for you. If you don't see anything for scholastics, try sending an email to the President or Executive Director. They should be able to help you round up a chess coach.

If you live in a sparsely populated area, the truth is, it may be difficult to find a coach who lives anywhere near you. If this is your case, then an online school is likely to be your best choice.

Once you've decided to contact a coach, the coach is going to want to make an estimation of your child's chess strength. Be prepared for some of these questions:

1. What is your child's age?
2. How long has he been playing?
3. Does he play tournament chess?
4. How many tournament games has he played?
5. Does your child have a USCF rating?
6. If so, what is it?

7. Is his rating rising, or has it fallen significantly recently?

The coach may have other questions, and you should start to get a feel as to whether this coach is someone you and your child will be comfortable with, no small consideration. Here are some questions you can ask the coach:

1. How long have you been coaching?
2. How long have you been coaching kids my child's age?
3. Why do you coach?
4. What's your chess rating?
5. How often will you meet with my child?
6. What is your fee?
7. Is it per lesson, or is there a monthly fee?
8. Can we meet once for free, to see how it might work out? Not all coaches will agree to the "free" part (after all his time and knowledge are his money makers), but you might be able to negotiate a lower price for the initial "consultation."

If you plan to call other coaches, feel free to mention this to the coach, and that you'll get back to him.

Chess Camps

Chess camps are like any "skills" camp, baseball, basketball, volleyball, and focus on helping the attendee become a stronger player. Many camps bring in chess teachers of some renown, including grandmasters. Your state chess organization is the place to start when searching for a chess camp for your player. Like any activity, it's wise to be certain your child wants to attend a camp, whether chess or some other sport. Forcing a child to go to a camp when he's reluctant to go for whatever reason, is not doing him or you any favors. Depending on your child's age, and whether he's been away from home for a week or so, perhaps for the first one you could try a "day" camp, where he goes during the day, but comes home at night, just like school.

Chapter 4 – Computer Chess

Earlier, I talked about using a computer as a tool to strengthen your child's play. I'd like to tell a story to illustrate another way you can use the computer. When my son was about six he became fascinated by the game. We played when we could, but there were times when I couldn't sit down and play a game with him. We had a stand-alone chess computer, the kind with real pieces versus being on the computer screen. The computer used a matrix to know which piece you moved (you pressed down on the square holding the piece, then pressed down on the landing square), and it used lights to tell you what its move was.

I set Nate up on one side, then told the computer to play itself, with Nate moving the pieces. In this way, he was able to see a well-played game, but be actively involved. I told him to guess what the computer would move. He played many games like this, and I knew it was working when he started asking me to come over and look at the board, and explain why the computer moved a certain piece.

The same can be achieved by using computer software. Whether you want to set up a physical board is up to you, but I recommend it. There's just something about a physical set that helps. Perhaps it's similar to the reason writers always edit on paper, you just see things better. The advantage to using computer software is that you can tell your child the same thing about guessing the next move. With computer software, your child can tell it to pause, thus giving him more time to work out a solution, on the physical board and set, then after deciding, tell it to play again. He will find out if he selected the same move as the computer.

As for software, well there's quite a lot to choose from. I've already mentioned Chessmaster, but here's a very short list and their prices as of 2010. Others that are available are much more expensive.

Computer Chess Software

- Chessmaster: The Art of Learning – Grandmaster Edition $24.95
- Fritz 12 – $59.95

It's possible to play chess by downloading some free software, but it may only be able to play games, and not do any analysis, or save the games.

Play live online

There are many sites that allow people to play against each other. I urge extreme caution in using an online game site and if the site has chat capability, I *do not recommend it for children of any age* **without parental supervision**. You must always be cognizant of the need to protect your child from predators. You cannot "know" for certain who is on the other end of the computer link.

Chapter 5 – Chess Clubs and Coaching

In this chapter we'll discuss how you can get a chess club started at your school, even if you can't be present for the club meetings. All that's needed is a desire to make it happen.

If your child is home schooled, there is likely a Home School Association. Contact them in place of a school principal. In 2009 I started coaching chess for just such an association and have 16 players.

Organizing a club

Most schools, especially high schools, have a chess club. If your child's school doesn't have a chess club, and you want to start one, you should prepare for a meeting, either in person or by phone, with the principal. There are four things a club must have:

- Players
- Place
- Equipment
- Coach

Here's a list of things you should have ready or should do prior to the meeting:

1. If you plan to do the coaching yourself, list why you want to coach and your chess coaching experience. If you don't have coaching experience, list your chess *playing* experience, or other teaching or volunteer activities.
2. If you don't have a coach, you can locate a chess coach volunteer by contacting your state chess association. Many cities have chess players who are retired and volunteer to coach chess. Some coach at more than one school.
3. Some schools already have some chess equipment. However, it's often not the kind of set and board that works well for teaching chess. The boards should have algebraic notation on them. Be prepared to help the school obtain tournament-style chess sets and boards. The United States Chess Foundation has a program that provides some free sets and boards. All that is needed is for a school representative to fill out a request form.
4. What age group do you want to invite to the chess club? If you're coaching, you can answer this yourself, but if you have enlisted the aid of a coaching volunteer, he / she can help you decide on this. I prefer to open it to all students (this is an issue only in schools with the lower grades as a part of their population: K – 3). Very young children can certainly learn and play chess, and play it well. However, you may require help managing younger children due to attention span and behavior differences as compared to students in grade four and up. Again, if you're coaching, you'll know what you want to accomplish. If you have a coach volunteer, ask him.
5. Gather information (studies) about the benefits of playing chess (you can use what I have on page 5 and / or 165).

When you have this information ready, make the call or attend a meeting with the principal. During the meeting, just tell the principal you would love to help his school start up a chess club. State whether you're willing to coach, or that you've acquired a coach volunteer. Continue making your pitch, although the principal may immediately become excited and tell you right off, "Thank you!" And ask you what he can do to help. From this point on, everything is gravy and the next steps are:

1. Determine a start date (have a few dates in mind and be sure to coordinate with your chess coach).
2. If a school sponsor (teacher) is required to be present (but not act as the coach), the principal will need to set that up. Teachers who work as sponsors are often paid, and this is up to the principal to arrange.
3. Advertise the club (see the next section).
4. Get copies of all materials (coordinate with your chess coach).
5. Obtain the equipment. If you are planning on getting equipment from the U.S. Chess Foundation, be sure to allow enough time for their processing. It could be up to six weeks before your sets arrive.
6. Tell the principal that parents should "sign up" their child ahead of time. This way you'll know about how many players to expect.
7. Be sure to ask the principal who you should work with at the school.

Advertising the club

Most schools send home newsletters or letters specific to an upcoming activity. I write the letter myself and ask the school to send it home. Here's an example of a letter from 2009. Feel free to use any part of this letter.

Dear Parents,

I'm pleased and grateful to be your chess coach. I wanted to introduce myself, so you'll know who's teaching your child(ren) chess.

I began playing tournament chess in 1987 and started coaching kids in 1991 when my son was in the first grade. Our rural Kansas elementary school team won two second place finishes at the state championship tournament playing against much larger schools. I am a United States Chess Federation Certified Coach. To earn this certification, I obtained an endorsement from a National Level Coach and passed a test on the topic "Scholastic Chess."

I strongly believe in the power of chess for kids. Many studies show a direct correlation between playing chess regularly and improved grades. One thing that I've noticed in my coaching years that isn't mentioned in the studies is that kids who play chess often have increased self-confidence and self-esteem. These intangibles cannot be measured directly by tests, but can affect directly how a child perceives his or her ability to take a test.

Chess appeals to people of all ages, gender, and professions. I've played tournament games against truck drivers, doctors, lawyers, ministers, accountants, government employees, computer programmers, teachers, and PhDs. Chess is a great equalizer: girls defeat boys; a child small in stature defeats a larger child; a younger player defeats an older player. I could go on and on, but you get the idea.

Today's students often have very busy schedules. (Ever feel like a chauffeur? Yep, done that.) It was my experience, and I knew of many other coaches who had similar experiences, while coaching chess for elementary and high school students, that chess was only a part of the students' lives. Many also played sports; baseball, football, basketball, and most were starters on their teams. Many were good students, some outstanding, others struggled in school, but regardless, they all loved chess and played well enough to win games at tournaments.

I look forward to teaching chess to your child(ren). I'll be providing some handouts to your child(ren) for the first three or four meetings. Ask your child to show them to you.

My goal is to teach the game, the expected good sportsmanship, and above all else, to make learning and playing chess fun! Please feel free to call me any time you have questions.

Yours in chess,

Ronn Munsterman
United States Chess Federation Certified Coach

Benefits of playing chess or Why your child(ren) should play chess, and regularly

- Chess players learn chess and enjoy a lifetime of playing, whether just for fun or in tournaments.

- Chess players improve their logical thinking process. Studies show that students who play chess regularly can improve their grades.

- Chess players improve their self-esteem and self-confidence.

- Chess players learn the value of decision making and the consequences, good and bad, of those choices.

- Chess players learn the process of short and long range planning which helps them prepare for adult everyday life.

- Chess players learn sportsmanship, which is the fundamental basis of all chess etiquette rules.

- Chess players experience the excitement of individual and team successes, sharing camaraderie.

- Chess players who attend tournaments meet chess players from all over, making new and close friendships.

- Chess players are intellectually challenged whether at home playing teammates or at tournaments.

Other steps

Quality, tournament-style chess equipment is available through many websites. I personally prefer to buy from the USCF's online store. The prices are competitive and some of the money goes to support chess in the United States. But what kind of equipment and supplies should you have? Here's a list, organized by whether you'll need it immediately or can obtain it later.

Need immediately

- Chess sets and boards (algebraic notation). See the section Asking for Free Equipment on the next page.
- A box big enough to haul the equipment around. I once used a plastic storage tub, but discovered that a rolling travel suitcase with a long handle made it all much easier. Mine easily holds ten sets and boards.
- Name tags.
- A Sharpie (for the name tags).
- The latest edition of USCF's *Official Rules of Chess*.
- Any handouts you're planning to use.

Can be obtained later

- Chess clocks. See section Asking for Money on page 167.
- Score sheets or score books.
- Pencils (for scorekeeping).

Optional equipment / supplies

- Demonstration board. This is a large (usually 28x28 inches) hanging board with plastic or magnetic pieces).
- Chess books. The general rule of thumb about chess books is that you should not purchase them for the club, instead, if you have some, take them as needed, but return them to your home. Chess books at clubs have a

tendency to get misplaced or "borrowed" for an extended period.

Asking for Free Equipment

The U.S. Chess Trust has a terrific program: Chess-For-Youth program (http://www.uschesstrust.com/programs-and-resources/chess-for-youth-program/). The following is from their web site:

There are two components to the Chess-For-Youth program:
1. Provision of free chess equipment (limit of up to five free boards and sets) to help start your chess program.
2. Provisions of free USCF memberships (limit of ten memberships per school) for needy students who are attending a Title I school and have never been a USCF member before (see definition of Title I under Free Membership Program Criteria).

Members receive a catalog filled with hundreds of the most up-to-date products, access to tournament information in print and on the website, as well as the right to play in rated OTB (over-the-board) and correspondence chess tournaments.

Its simple to get involved with the Chess-For-Youth program. Simply have a school administrator or principal complete the required application , include a brief letter (on official letterhead) stating the request, and send it to the Chess-For-Youth Program, U.S. Chess Trust, PO Box 838,Wallkill, NY 12589.

The U.S. Chess Trust will review your request and if approved, will send up to five free chess sets and boards to support your program.

If you are requesting the 10 free memberships, then please include the name, gender, complete address, and complete birth date of each of the students.

Please allow 4-6 weeks for processing.

Asking for Money

There are several sources of funding for your chess club:
1. The school, or school board or school administration, depending on your district's organization. Ask your school's principal for guidance.
2. The parents. I've found many parents want to contribute something toward their child's chess learning.

3. Businesses. Some companies, large and small, are happy to support chess in the schools. If you have contacts with people in business, I suggest using those first, rather than "cold calling" a business.
4. Yourself. You can decide whether to contribute equipment in addition to your time.

Decide who you want to ask for money. There's nothing wrong with calling it what it is, no need to gloss it over or shine it up, but do what makes you comfortable.

How you go about asking is going to be based on your personal comfort and style. Regardless of that, though, I recommend a simple approach when asking for money, whether in person or a phone call, or in writing (although I prefer a face-to-face method):

1. Introduce yourself and be yourself. Remember to smile! Include your coaching background if you have one, or your chess playing background. If you are a USCF certified chess coach, be sure to mention that, both verbally and in writing.
2. Provide a handout with the information noted below. Be sure your contact information is on the handout.
3. Say that you're starting up a new club.
4. Give the name of the chess club and what school it's associated with.
5. State the benefits of chess for kids (point out a few, but put the full version of it in the handout).
6. State that you're here to request money for (tell them exactly what you are planning to buy) and tell them how much.
7. If they are not going to make an immediate decision, they should tell you. Feel free to ask when you might hear from them.
8. Thank them for their time.

Once you receive their answer, be sure to thank them in writing, regardless of their answer. Even if the reply was "no," being courteous marks you as professional, and next year, the answer could be "yes."

Local Chess Clubs

In addition to a school club, or if one isn't available, you can locate chess clubs through both your state chess association and the USCF. Chess players tend to be welcoming, and finding a club where your child can play, even if it's against adults, can lead to a terrific, and lasting, chess experience for you and your child.

Chapter 6 – Coaching Tips

Every coach I've ever had the pleasure to meet and know over the years, always had one thing as their center focus: to promote chess for kids. We've already talked about why kids should play chess, however, if you've decided to take on the role of chess coach: thank you! I want to provide some ideas and tips that can make chess fun for the kids, and you. Every coach or teacher has his own style. This chapter is not about thrusting my style on you, although I certainly will mention a few things as do's and don'ts.

The first meeting and subsequent meetings

Often, the first meeting is attended by players and their parents, and sometimes someone from the school. First of all, be yourself, but have a plan of what you want to say. Tell them a little about yourself: what you do for a living, where you live, your family; then tell them about your chess background: when you started playing, why you love the game, whether you've coached before, and if so, where, and mention things like how well your team did at tournaments.

I recommend having name stickers for the players. Be sure to tell them what you want them to call you. Is it Mr., Ms., or Mrs., or as I prefer, "Coach?" I prefer they don't call me by my first name. I am the coach, not their classmate.

After the introduction, I tell them what my goals are for them every week. Those goals are:

1. Have fun.
2. Learn to play chess *correctly*.
3. Become a stronger player *each* week.

Let's discuss these goals.

Have fun: chess is a game. A game, by definition, should be fun for the players. That doesn't mean it can't be difficult. Chess is perhaps the most difficult board game ever devised to play well. Focus on having fun, and learning while you're at it.

Learn to play chess correctly: I've coached plenty of kids who, when we first met, said they can play chess, but as we progress through some exercises and begin to play, it's clear someone, maybe a relative or a best friend has taught them things that are incorrect. A simple example is we know that a pawn only captures on the diagonal, but a player was taught that the pawn captures straight ahead! We have to undo those incorrect teachings. Playing correctly doesn't include just the rules, it includes playing sound, tactically accurate games.

Become a stronger player each week: Each lesson should include two things:

1. A review of some of the previous week's material / concepts.
2. Introduce new information. The new information can be things like tactics (pins, for example) shown on a board or demonstration board, and / or information about the chess world, for example, talk about Grandmasters. Bring in photos of a few and talk about them as people.

In the first meeting, you'll need to ask whether your students have played chess. You should also ask of those who say they've played if anyone has a chess rating. If they look at you like you just spoke in a foreign language, the answer is no. We'll come back to rated players in a moment, but for now, let's say none of the players have ratings. If you have some players who have played and some who have not, you need to be prepared to have two classes. I recommend you have those students who have played set up boards and play on one side of the room, and the new-to-chess students join you on the other side.

You may need to plan to have two separate classes like this for many weeks. The best way to handle this is get each group playing while you teach the other group. You may have to repeat material this way, but it's best for the players. Here's a sample lesson plan to illustrate this idea.

New Players Group

1. Introduce board, files a-h, ranks 1-8.
2. Show proper board position.
3. Introduce the pieces' names and their point values along with the demo board (if you have one) pieces.
   a. pawns
   b. Bishops
   c. Rooks
   d. Queen
   e. King
   f. Knight
4. Hold up pieces at random and get the class to say the name and point value.
5. Discuss captures in general including protecting another piece.
6. Pawn placement, moves and captures
7. Introduce sportsmanship – shake hands before game, say "Good Luck."

Get the players started playing the pawn game and move over to teach the experienced players. If players finish before time is up, they can switch colors and play again.

Experienced Players Group

Play games while you are teaching the new players. Then you can cover the following material while the new players are playing.

Suggested Topics (over several weeks)

1. Piece names and point values. I've had players who came to me and knew how to play, but were completely unaware of piece value.
2. The algebraic board.
3. Chess notation from Lesson 4.
4. Checkmate patterns from Lesson 5.
5. Tactics
    a. Pins
    b. Skewers
    c. Discovered check

One thing I've done is cover items 1 through 3 at the same time for both groups to save time and get everyone to the same point.

Get them to the boards right away

The sooner you can get your players to the board, the better. Even during instruction time, the boards should be set up and ready to go.

End of the class

Here are the things you should do at the end of each class:
1. Summarize what was covered. You can do this with all groups at the same time.
2. If you know what you're covering the next week, give them a brief overview.
3. Have the players put the equipment away and clean up after themselves.

Funner games

You know how some games just seem to draw kids to them? Blitz and bughouse chess are by far the most sought after "recreational" play of chess you'll find among kids, and adults love them too.

Blitz (speed) chess

Speed chess is just like it sounds: a game where players play fast. Generally, the game clock is set to five minutes for each player. All the regular rules apply except for touch-move. You can move a piece, let go of it, but until you hit the clock, you can take it back and move something else.

Bughouse chess

Bughouse chess is speed chess with partners, two to a team. To someone watching, it will look chaotic. Same rules as Blitz with these add-ons:
- Teammates play opposite colors and sit side-by-side.
- When one player captures an opponent's piece, he passes it to his partner.
- If the partner has lost the same piece, he may pick up the captured piece and place it on his board, anywhere, even to call check, *instead of moving.*
- Teammates can tell each other they need a certain piece.
- The game ends when one player is checkmated, loses on time, or makes an illegal move and is caught.

Tag Team Chess

This is a game I made up that the kids loved playing. A team is made up of two players. If you have an odd number of kids, make one team three.
- quick chess, 10 minutes on the clock.
- partner is at the far end of the room.
- after about 2 minutes the coach calls "tag" and the player at the board crawls (if you have a big enough room, they can run) to his partner, tags him and the partner runs or crawls back to play until the next "tag" is called.

Team Chess

This game forces players to analyze a board that is quite different from the last time they saw it. They see the board with "fresh" eyes, and it shows them possibilities they may not have seen if they'd been playing the game all along. It also exposes to the players that while they may have seen an opportunity and made a move to start a nice attacking sequence, the player immediately behind them did not see the follow-up moves, and so the attack fizzled. Another part of analysis this game uncovers for the players is they also had to constantly check the piece count to see whether their team was up, down, or even in material. This deepened their understanding of the position.

1. Divide your players into groups of roughly equal strength (I had two teams of six players). If you have a lot of players, just have more teams.
2. Set up one board for each pair of teams. I selected a captain for each team – the strongest player on the team.
3. Use clocks if you have them; I used G/10. The captains face off at the board, with their teammates standing off to the side (so they can see the board).
4. The captains make the first move, hit the clock, then they get up and go to the end of their team's line, and the next player sits down.
5. This continues until the game ends on the board or a flag falls.

Rotation Chess

The purpose of this game, like Team Chess, is to teach players to analyze a position. Since they didn't create the position, they will have to take time to figure out what's going on before moving. This really helps players learn that necessary skill of "analysis before making a move." Be prepared for some grumbling from players who inherit a weak position!

This is not speed chess, but if you have clocks, you can set them to about 15 minutes each. You need to let the players know in which direction they will be rotating.

1. Have your players take a seat at a board.
2. They start the clocks and begin play.
3. After about two or three minutes, you call "rotate."
4. Each player gets up and moves to the board on his *right*. There will be two players without a board on their right. They go all the way to their left to the now-empty board.

Club Tournaments

It's relatively easy to set up a tournament for your club. I've conducted speed chess tournaments that the kids love. You will need clocks for this. You can use a Round Robin style called "Quads" where groups of four play each other once. I've also used Swiss Pairings (manually, for small groups) and a bracketed style tournament similar to College Baseball with double elimination.

The *Official Rules of Chess* provides information on how to run various types of tournaments. Just plan to have a lot of fun.

Club Ladder

Many chess clubs, adult and scholastic alike, have a Club Ladder. My players always enjoy issuing and defending against challenges. This is a ranking of the members based on games played at the club. Here are the Club Ladder rules I use:
1. The original player position on the ladder can be determined by:
   a. USCF rating, if any
   b. points earned so far in any club tournaments,
      i. tie-breaks
         1. opponents' accumulative score
         2. head-to-head
         3. alphabetical order.
2. Challenges are issued by players in the order determined for that week, either bottom-up, or top-down.
3. The first week, the order of challenges is from bottom to top. The second week, the order is reversed and goes top to bottom. It alternates each week thereafter.

4. When the challenge order is up, you may challenge anyone **above** you on the ladder.
5. When the challenge order is down, you may challenge anyone **below** you on the ladder.
6. New players are placed at the bottom of the ladder.
7. If you don't show up two weeks in a row, you drop half the distance to the bottom, then if a third week in a row is missed, you go to the bottom of the ladder. You can relax this rule if the player advises you she'll be gone, like for a vacation.

Results

- Both players record the score of the game on the "Pairings - Club Ladder Games" sheet and tell Coach.
- If the higher person wins, there is no change.
- If the game is a draw, the lower rated player moves up to the spot just below the higher player.
- If the higher person loses, the challenger takes the higher player's spot and the higher player moves down one spot.
- For Ladder games, the touch-move rule is in effect.
- The time limit is no less than G/15.
- If your flag falls, you lose **unless** your opponent does not have mating material, which results in a draw.
    - Draw if your opponent has:
        - King only
        - King and Knight only
        - King and Bishop only.

Tournaments

There will come a point where either you or your players or your players' parents may decide it's time to start playing in tournaments. The first thing I'd like to say on this subject is that you should be bringing up tournaments at opportune moments throughout meetings. For example, if you played in one recently, tell your players how it went. Show them a game or parts of games.

The second thing is that you should use the tournament checklist to determine which players are ready to play. My goal was to always make sure all players were ready, so no one would feel excluded.

Two key things in that checklist are being familiar with using a clock, and keeping score because both are required for most tournaments. I can't overemphasize how important these skills are.

Criticizing the move, not the player

At the risk of sounding too soft-hearted, it's very important when coaching kids, especially those who are in grade five and below, to be careful when criticizing a move choice made by a player. Whether you are playing the child yourself, or going over a game he played, a player is likely to associate a criticism of the move as an extended criticism of him. First, as a matter of semantics, I label moves as one of these types:

- Strong: improves your position, and weakens your opponent's
- Weak: hurts your position, and strengthens your opponent's
- Neutral: neither helps nor hurts your position. One can argue that a neutral move is really weak since it does not strengthen your position, and weaken your opponent's.

Personally (and I know many coaches who agree), I never call a move a "bad" move, but I pull no punches in calling a move "weak."

Whenever I'm working with a student, I prefer to ask questions like those below because they provide the student the opportunity to analyze the move away from the pressure of a game in progress.

"Why did you choose this move?"

Sometimes, these questions will provoke the answer with which parents and coaches the world over are all too familiar: "I don't know," or a shrug. If you think that's the best you're going to get, move on, but if you think the player is just trying to duck the question, it's okay to pry a little, but you'll have to use leading questions:

"Did you see another move you chose not to make?"

"Is the move you chose the strongest one in this position?"

"I see a stronger move than this one, can you find it?"

You'll have to work with the players over time to get them to understand that it's okay to say they chose the weakest move by mistake, whether by calculating incorrectly, or moving too fast (the biggest culprit). It's also okay to ask if they think the move was a blunder. We all make blunders in our chess life. If that's what it is, you can ask if they know how they blundered, but I can almost guarantee the cause will be moving too fast, a "reaction" move, rather than one made after thought and calculation.

Coaching after a win is easy, after a loss not so, or Over coaching – this isn't football

As parents, we've all seen the look: head down, bottom lip stuck out, arms hanging limp. It's the famous dejected look. No matter the game, it appears. In my experience, few young players are able to avoid this outward, obvious display of a lost game. As they gain experience, and have won a few games, they come to understand on their own terms that losing a game isn't a catastrophe.

On the opposite side, when a player returns to the team table after a win, it's going to be with a quick step, and a wide grin.

How should you handle both? I recommend making a big deal out of the win. A high five is always in order, along with a "Good job!"

The loss is different. I downplay it. I say, "That's okay, there'll be another one." Usually, the player recovers pretty quickly, especially if one of his teammates sits with him. It doesn't matter whether the teammate won or lost his own game, just being with another player helps. I often ask one or both of these questions: "Do you think you played your best?" or "Do you know where the game was lost?" You'd be surprised by some of the answers. Often an answer to the first question includes an answer to the second. For example he might say, "I played really well up until move 26, then I moved my Knight to the wrong square and he got the advantage. If I'd have moved it to–" and he'll name a different square, "I'd still be playing."

Seriously, I've had players, even relatively new players say something like that. This is a coaching heaven moment. There is no need to go over the game with this player. As an aside, I rarely went over the game with a player right after the game, in between rounds (our time control was G30, so there wasn't much time), I found it was generally better for the players to relax and visit with their friends and family instead. This is your call, and some players may benefit from game analysis.

Communicating

You should plan on communicating effectively with many groups. These groups are:
- players
- parents
- school administrator(s)
- other chess coaches
- tournament directors
- USCF staff

Be straightforward when you communicate. If using humor is in your skill set, use it.

Thanking the parents

Parents often provide various kinds of help to you the coach; driving kids to tournaments, providing equipment, helping out during club meetings. Always be sure to thank them often and in front of the players.

USCF Certified Chess coach program

The USCF sponsors a program for chess coaches. Here is the information from the USCF web site:

The USCF Certified Chess Coach Program has been designed to aid the average Scholastic Chess Coach in their endeavors. For many years many school districts have not paid Chess Coaches because they compared Chess coaches to athletic coaches. Athletic coaches are required to go through training and/or testing to be paid as a coach and Chess coaches are not.

This program is to insure that Chess coaches have a basic level of knowledge necessary to coach children in Chess so that a school district can know they are hiring a knowledgeable person to coach the district's / school's children.

The purpose of this program is to provide that level of testing to make sure that your school district will know that you have reached a certain level of competency in Chess as certified by the United States Chess Federation. There are five levels of the Certified Chess Coach Program:
- Local Chess Coach (Level I)
- Intermediate Chess Coach (Level II)
- Advanced Chess Coach (Level III)
- National Chess Coach (Level IV)
- Professional Chess Coach (Level V)

Each level has different requirements and you can investigate them on the web site. Some of the requirements are to pass a written test and garner endorsement letter(s) from other chess coaches.

Chapter 7 – Resources

Books

U.S. Chess Federation's Official Rule of Chess

This is the rule book used by all USCF sanctioned tournaments. As I mentioned earlier, it's a sizable book, but it's worth reading if you want to be serious about tournament chess. For coaches, it should be required reading because you must know what to teach your players about playing in tournaments.

Attacking Chess: Aggressive Strategies and Inside Moves from the U.S. Junior Chess Champion – Josh Waitzkin

This is an excellent book where Josh shows and explains many of the strongest attacks a player can use.

Web

United States Chess Federation
www.uschess.org

Chess Games
www.chessgames.com

This is a great chess game research study tool. You can search games by many criteria, including year, player, and opening. It has a Java chess board display where you can play the game one move at a time as well as see the entire game in chess notation. You can also copy the game notation and paste it into a document for use in class.

Movies

Many movies contain actors playing a game of chess. Almost always, the scene involves one character making a move and chirruping triumphantly, "checkmate." However, few movies are *about* chess. Two standout films expose the viewers to the world of tournament chess, the players, and their families. I highly recommend you watch both of these with your child, or if you're coaching, with your team.

Searching for Bobby Fischer
Editorial Review – Amazon.com
Steve Zaillian, the Oscar-winning screenwriter of Schindler's List, made his directorial debut with this critically acclaimed but little-seen drama based on the nonfiction book by Fred Waitzkin, about a father (Joe Mantegna) who discovers that his seven-year-old son (Max Pomeranc) is a genius at playing chess. The boy plays chess for fun, but when he's tutored by a former champion (Ben Kingsley) and entered into high-pressure competitions, an enjoyable pastime becomes a source of tension and resentment, forcing the father to reconsider his parental priorities. A poignant study of the difference between parental idealism and proper parenting, the movie is also an observantly witty portrait of a precocious child who is still, after all, a child, and still eager for the joyful discoveries of youth. While offering a fascinating look into the world of competitive chess, the movie's dramatically engrossing and extremely well-acted by a brilliant cast that also includes David Paymer, William H. Macy, and Dan Hedaya in memorable supporting roles. – Jeff Shannon

Knights of the South Bronx

Editorial Review – Amazon.com

Under-funded schools with a large percentage of poverty-ridden students often find it difficult to provide a high quality education, but sometimes it just takes one special teacher to spark the interests and intellects of an entire classroom of children. Richard Mason (Ted Danson), a white-haired, recently unemployed businessman, decides to revive his long-dormant passion for teaching by accepting a substitute teaching position at a poverty ridden public school in the South Bronx. Thrown into a fourth-grade classroom, Mr. Mason is at first doubtful of his ability to positively impact a classroom of students that include a smart-mouthed, seemingly stupid boy named Jimmy (Malcom David Kelley), a crack-addict's daughter Kenya (Keke Palmer), French immigrant M.D. (Yves Michel-Beneche), and Kindergartner Dawson (Antonio Ortiz) who has no place to go but his sister's classroom once his half-day Kindergarten class finishes for the day. When student Jimmy stumbles upon Mr. Mason in the park one weekend, he discovers that his teacher is a brilliant chess player and becomes completely intrigued by the game. Suddenly, Mr. Mason realizes that the game of chess might just provide a whole new way to reach a classroom full of unwilling students. Soon, his students are showing up early for school in order to play chess, participating in class, and even doing their homework. As Mr. Mason encourages his students to perfect their games and enter a local chess tournament, each child's sense of self-worth grows as do their test scores in all subjects. Ultimately, the children become superior chess players as well as firm believers that if they refuse to give in to anger and use their intellect, they can become just about anything they want to be. Based on the true experience of David MacEnulty, Knights of the South Bronx is a well-acted, potent presentation about the power of intellect and self-confidence. (Ages 8 and older with parental guidance) – Tami Horiuchi

Chapter 8 – A short rules list for tournament players

This chapter highlights a few rules players and coaches should know before attending a tournament. I recommend you buy a copy of the *Official Rules of Chess* if you are planning to attend tournaments. I paraphrased the rules to simplify them for the students. The exact rule name and number from the *Official Rules of Chess* is noted for your reference.

Whenever a player wants to invoke one of these, or any rule from the rule book, he should stop both clocks and contact a tournament director. Generally, in scholastic tournaments, all a player needs to do is hold up his hand and a director or a coach will help him.

Annoying behavior prohibited – Rule 20G

Making annoying noises, whether on purpose or not, is not allowed. Some examples are talking, humming, finger/pencil tapping, and foot tapping.

Draw on insufficient material to continue – Rule 14D

This occurs when the following conditions exist:
- King vs. King
- King vs. King with Bishop or Knight
- King and Bishop vs. King and Bishop, with Bishops on diagonals of the same color.

Draw on insufficient material to win on time – Rule 14E

This is the exception to the rule that says when you run out of time, you lose. If a player's time has run out, and his opponent has only the material listed here, the game is a draw, not a loss for the player whose time ran out.
- King
- King with Bishop or Knight
- King with two Knights and there is no forced win.

Draw on triple occurrence of position – Rule 14C

This is a tough one for new players. What the rule means is that the board looks the same three times, but it does not have to be on consecutive moves. The best way to explain this to your student is if we took a picture of the board during the game, would three pictures be exactly the same, with *all* pieces in the same place? If the answer is yes, then you can claim a draw. With few exceptions, the player making the claim must have a score sheet to show to the director to back up the claim.

Illegal move in sudden death – Rule 11D

If the time control is sudden death, a player makes and completes by hitting the clock, an illegal move, his opponent is entitled to an additional two minutes of time added to his clock. In order to do this, the player entitled to the extra time should point out the illegal move, stop the clock, and call for a director.

Incorrect initial position – Rule 11F

New and experienced players alike sometimes set up their boards incorrectly. Some examples are white playing from rows 7 and 8, instead of 1 and 2; Kings and Queens on the wrong starting squares, the board is turned sideways. If, before the completion of black's 10th move, it's discovered that the board was set up incorrectly, or the players are playing the wrong colors, then the game must be restarted from the correct position and colors. If clocks are in use, the amount of time run off for each player remains in play.

If the mistake is discovered after black's 10th move, the game continues as-is.

Appendix A – Chess Glossary

active – a piece is active when it can participate in attacks and defense.

algebraic notation – a board location notation in which the ranks (rows) are numbered from 1 to 8, and the files are lettered from 'a' (leftmost) to 'h' (rightmost), and squares are "named" by their file letter followed by their row number: For example: e4, c3. See: **board**.

attack – when a piece can move to a square, it is said to attack that square; also the act of attacking with one or more pieces. See: **combination**.

back rank (row) – the rank containing the King's starting square.

backward – toward the player's back rank. See: **forward**.

battery – two or more pieces supporting each other on the same file or row. Typically refers to the Rooks, but includes Queen and Rook(s).

Bishop – Usually designed with a "hat" shaped somewhat like a Catholic Cardinal. Moves on the diagonal and always remains on the same color space as where it starts. Each side gets one light-squared and one dark-squared Bishop.

black – one of the two colors of chess spaces, pieces, and players. See: **color**, **white**.

board – the playing surface for the game. Comprised of 64 equal-sized square spaces, 8 by 8. The rows are called ranks, and the columns are called files. The spaces are alternately dark and light as one moves up a file, or across a rank. The right-hand corner square of the board is white for both players. See: **algebraic notation**.

book – moves that are regarded as standard or expected for a particular opening or sequence. So called because the moves appear in many chess books. See: **variation**.

capture – when a piece is moved to a space occupied by an opposing piece, the opposing piece is "captured," and removed from play. See: **exchange**.

castle – a special move involving the King and one of the Rooks. Also: an informal alternate name for a Rook. See: **castle long**, **castle short**, **Rook**.

castle long – castling involving the Queen's Rook.

castle short – castling involving the King's Rook.

castling on opposite sides – when one player castles short and the other castles long.

center – the four center spaces: d4, d5, e4, and e5.

check – an attack on the opposing King. See: **checkmate**, **double check**, **discovered check**.

checkmate – trapping the opposing King so that he cannot move anywhere without moving into check, the attacking piece cannot be blocked, and / or captured. See: **check**, **trap**.

chess clock – a special clock used in timed chess games. It has two clocks in the same body and may be analog or digital. If analog, it will have a device called a **flag**, that indicates a player's time has run out. If digital, the clock runs down to zero.

clock – short for chess clock. See: **chess clock**.

color – chess pieces are called white or black regardless of the actual color of the pieces. Color also refers to the players, as in the white player or the black player as denoted by which color of pieces they are playing with. See: **black**, **white**.

combination – attacking with more than one piece, as in a coordinated attack. Often leads to forced moves by the opponent and an advantage in material or space for the attacker. See: **attack**.

correspondence chess – chess played by postal or electronic mail.

descriptive notation – an older notation where the files are referred to by the side of the board (Queen's or King's) along with the type of piece on the first rank at the beginning of the game (Rook, Knight, Bishop). The ranks are referred to by the names 1 to 8 as with algebraic notation, but the counting is relative to the starting rank of the player. Each space will have two names: one when referred to by black, and another when referred to by white.

development – moves that activate pieces, especially toward the opposite player's pieces. See: **active**.

diagonal – squares aligned at the angle. Squares on a diagonal are the same color.

discovered check – check that occurs when one piece moves out of the way of a piece that now can call check, but could not before the move.

double check – when a piece moves and calls check, and another piece that was previously blocked from calling check by the moved piece, now calls check also. See: **check**, **discovered check**.

doubled pawns – two pawns of the same color on the same file. Generally considered to be a disadvantage because the trailing pawn cannot move.

draw –a game that ends with neither player in checkmate. Typically, draws are offered and accepted, but there are circumstances where a player may claim the game is drawn by rule, such as the triple occurrence repetition rule. A tie game earning each player a half-point. See: **stalemate**.

en passant – French for 'in passing.' A special pawn capture rule.

endgame – one of the three parts of the game. The endgame is defined as when there are few pieces left on the board.

exchange – occurs when one piece is captured, then the capturing piece is immediately captured. See: **capture**.

exchange, down in the – when a player gives up more material than he got during a piece exchange. Example: opponent's Knight is captured at the loss of a Rook or Queen.

exchange, even – when each player gains and loses the same amount of material. For example: each player gives up a Rook.

exchange, up in the – when a player gains more material than he lost during a piece exchange. Example: Opponent's Rook is captured at the loss of a Knight or a Bishop.

fianchetto – when a Bishop moves from its starting square onto one of the long diagonals, for example: b2, g2, b7, and g7.

FIDE – French acronym for the World Chess Federation (Fédération Internationale des Échecs).

flag – the time forfeit indicator on an analog chess clock.

forced mate – a sequence of forced moves leading up to checkmate.

forced move – occurs when the opponent has limited choices, and the best move is forced upon him.

forward – toward the opponent's back rank. See: **backward**.

four-move checkmate – another name for scholar's mate.

gambit – an opening involving the offer of a pawn sacrifice.

half-open file – a file with only one pawn on it. See: **open file**.

isolated pawn – a pawn that does not have any neighboring friendly pawns.

King – the most important piece on the board. He cannot be captured. When he is trapped, it is checkmate. Typically designed with a crown-like shaped hat, and a cross on the top.

Kingside – on the half of the board containing the King's starting square. Files 'e' to 'h.' See: **Queenside**.

Knight – a piece shaped like a horse. The only one that can jump over other pieces.

line – a row, file, or diagonal. Also: the line of play, as in the sequence of moves is the line taken.

lose – to be defeated by an opponent through checkmate, or to resign the game. See: **checkmate**, **resign, win**.

lose the exchange – See: **exchange, down in the**.

luft – a square left open in front of the King to prevent checkmate on the back rank.

major pieces – Queens and Rooks.

mate – short for checkmate. See: **checkmate**.

material – another name for chess pieces.

mating attack – an attack that could lead to checkmate.

middle game – one of the three parts of the game. It is defined generally as starting after the point when both players have positioned their pieces in the opening, usually including the development of the Knights and Bishops, and castling.

minor pieces – Knights and Bishops.

move – when a player moves one of his own pieces to another square. Also: phrase for whose "move" or turn it is, as in "It's your move."

open file – a file containing no pawns of either color. See: **half-open file**.

opening – the first moves in the game, where the focus is usually on controlling the center, developing of the pieces, and castling.

opponent – white is the opponent of black and vice-versa.

pairings – the assignment of opponents during a tournament. See: **round robin, Swiss pairings**.

passed pawn – a pawn that has no opposing pawns on the files next to its own, and none in front of it. Can no longer be blocked or captured by opposing pawns.

pawn – the lowest valued piece. Typically designed with a round knob on its top.

perpetual check – occurs when one player calls check on every move and the opponent is powerless to stop it. Leads to a draw. See: **draw**.

piece – a game-piece that is not a pawn, although, generally, piece refers to all of the game-pieces.

pin – a piece is pinned when it is attacked by an opposing piece and on the attacking line behind the pinned piece is another piece of a higher value (or the King – when it would be illegal to move the pinned piece).

play – play the game of chess.

promotion – when a pawn reaches the opponent's back rank (the pawn's 8th row), it can be promoted to any other piece except a King.

Queen – the most powerful piece on the board. Typically designed with a flat crown on top.

Queenside – on the half of the board containing the Queen's starting square. Files 'a' to 'd'. See: **Kingside**.

rating – a measurement of a player's strength relative to other rated players. In the Unites States, the USCF is responsible for the ratings calculations performed at the conclusion of a tournament.

resign – a player may quit the game and award his opponent a victory, or win. Players most often resign when it becomes apparent, even obvious, that they cannot win the game.

Rook – the second most powerful piece on the board. Typically shaped like a castle, thus is often called a "castle." See: **castling**.

round robin – a tournament pairing system where each player plays each of the other players once. See: **pairings, Swiss pairings**.

sacrifice – a purposeful loss of a piece in the interest of gaining some other advantage.

scholar's mate – mate in four moves using the Queen and Bishop. See: **four-move checkmate**.

space –.a square on the board.

square – one of the 64 squares on a chess board. Squares are either dark or light. See: **space**.

stalemate – a specific kind of draw (or tie). Occurs only when the player to move has no legal move, but is not in check. See: **draw**.

starting rank – the first row for each player, where all pieces except pawns start the game.

Swiss pairings – a tournament pairings system where players are ranked (by ratings) in descending order from top to bottom, then the top half is paired against the bottom half, in descending order. In subsequent rounds, players with the same score are put into score groups, and then split in half and paired. The purpose of the Swiss system is to allow winning players to rise to the top and be paired against other winning players.

tempo – when one side seems to have an advantage based on the timing of moves.

tie – See: **draw**.

time control – the amount of time each player has to make all of his moves. Some time controls are sudden-death (for example: G/60 limits each player to 60 minutes to make ALL moves), and others are so many moves in a specified amount time, then a sudden death time frame, for example: 40/90, SD60 means each player must make the first 40 moves within 90 minutes, then he will have an additional 60 minutes for the remainder of ALL of his moves; failure to make the first 40 in 90 minutes causes a loss on time.

tournament – an organized gathering of chess players who play each other for prizes and / or titles. Most tournaments are "rated." See: **rating**.

trap – a piece is trapped when it is threatened and the threat cannot be neutralized. Also, a series of moves by one player leading to an unfavorable position for the opponent.

turn – See: **move**.

United States Chess Federation (USCF) – the governing body for chess in the United States.

variation – generally refers to openings and identifies a possible line of moves that occurs at a certain point in the opening. See: **book**.

white – one of the two colors of chess spaces, pieces, and players. See: **color, black**.

win – to defeat an opponent, either by checkmate or when the opponent resigns. See: **checkmate, lose, resign**.

win the exchange – See: **exchange, up in the**.

zugzwang – German for 'compulsion to move.' Most commonly: When every possible move worsens a player's position. Also, when a player foregoes immediate capture of compensating material for a piece just lost, and instead creates a larger threat the enemy must respond to, eventually achieving material (and perhaps positional) compensation.

zwischenzug – German for an in-between move. Not quite the same as **zugzwang**. For example, in a King and Rook vs. King checkmate, sometimes the player with the Rook must move, but doesn't want to move his King, so he moves his Rook one square, forcing the opponent to move his King into a worse position that leads to checkmate. See **zugzwang**.

Appendix B – Famous Players

World Champions

Viswanathan Anand 2007–current (India)
Vladimir Kramnik 2000–2007 (Russia)
Garry Kasparov 1985–2000, U.S.S.R (Russia)
Anatoly Karpov 1975–1985, U.S.S.R (Russia)
Robert J. Fischer 1972–1975, (United States)
Boris Spassky 1969–1972, U.S.S.R (Russia)
Tigran Petrosian 1963–1969, U.S.S.R (Armenia)
Mikhail Tal 1960–1961, U.S.S.R (Latvia)
Vasily Smyslov 1957–1958, U.S.S.R (Russia)
Mikhail Botvinnik 1948–1957, 1958-1960, 1961-1963 (U.S.S.R, Russia)
Max Euwe 1935-1937 (Holland)
Alexander Alekhine 1927–1935, 1937-1946 (Russia/France)
Jose Raul Capablance 1921–1927 (Cuba)
Emanuel Lasker 1894–1921 (Germany)
Willhem Steinitz 1886–1894 (Austria)
Endnote [2]

U.S. Champions (Men)

2009: Hikaru Nakamura
2008: Yury Shulman
2007: Alexander Shabalov
2006: Alexander Onischuk
2005: Hikaru Nakamura
2003/4: Alexander Shabalov
2002: Larry Christiansen
2000: Joel Benjamin / Alexander Shabalov / Yasser Seirawan
1999: Boris Gulko
1998: Nick de Firmian
1997: Joel Benjamin
1996: Alex Yermolinsky
1995: Nick de Firmian / Patrick Wolff / Alexander Ivanov
1994: Boris Gulko
1993: Alexander Shabalov / Alex Yermolinsky
1992: Patrick Wolff
1991: Gata Kamsky
1990: Lev Alburt
1989: Roman Dzindzichashvili / Yasser Seirawan / Stuart Rachels
1988: Michael Wilder
1987: Nick de Firmian / Joel Benjamin
1986: Yasser Seirawan
1985: Lev Alburt
1984: Lev Alburt
1983: Walter Browne / Larry Christiansen/ Roman Dzindzichashvili
1981: Walter Browne / Yasser Seirawan
1980: Walter Browne / Larry Evans /Larry Christiansen
1978: Lubomir Kavalek
1977: Walter Browne
1975: Walter Browne
1974: Walter Browne
1973: John Grefe / Lubomir Kavalek
1972: Robert Byrne
1970: Samuel Reshevsky

1969: Samuel Reshevsky
1968: Larry Evans
1966: Bobby Fischer
1965: Bobby Fischer
1963: Bobby Fischer
1962: Bobby Fischer
1961: Larry Evans
1960: Bobby Fischer
1959: Bobby Fischer
1958: Bobby Fischer
1954: Arthur Bisguier
1951: Larry Evans
1948: Herman Steiner
1946: Samuel Reshevsky
1944: Arnold Denker
1942: Samuel Reshevsky
1940: Samuel Reshevsky
1938: Samuel Reshevsky
1936: Samuel Reshevsky
1909-1935: Frank Marshall
1906 - 1909: Jackson Showalter
1897 - 1906: Harry Nelson Pillsbury
1895 - 1897: Jackson Showalter
1894 - 1895: Albert Hodges
1894: Jackson Showalter
1891 - 1894: Solomon Lipschutz
1890 - 1891: Jackson Showalter
1871 - 1890: George H. Mackenzie
1857 - 1871: Paul Morphy
1845 - 1857: Charles Stanley
Endnote [3]

U.S. Champions (Women)

2009: Anna Zatonskih
2008: Anna Zatonskih
2007: Irina Krush
2006: Anna Zatonskih
2005: Rusudan Goletiani
2004: Jennifer Shahade
2003: Anna Hahn
2001/02: Jennifer Shahade
2000: Elina Groberman - Camilla Baginskaite
1999: Anjelina Belakovskaia
1998: Irina Krush
1997: Esther Epstein
1996: Anjelina Belakovskaia
1995: Anjelina Belakovskaia - Sharon Burtman
1994: Elena Donaldson
1993: Elena Donaldson - Irina Levitina
1992: Irina Levitina
1991: Esther Epstein - Irina Levitina
1990: Elena Donaldson
1989: Dr. Alexey (Rudolph) Root
1987: Anna Akhsharumova
1986: Inna Izrailov
1984: Diane Savereide
1981: Diane Savereide
1979: Rachel Crotto
1978: Diane Savereide - Rachel Crotto
1977: Diane Savereide - Rachel Crotto
1976: Diane Savereide
1975: Diane Savereide
1974: Mona May Karff
1972: Eva Aronson - Marilyn Koput
1969: Gisela Kahn Gresser
1967: Gisela Kahn Gresser
1966: Gisela Kahn Gresser - Lisa Lane
1965: Gisela Kahn Gresser
1964: Sonja Graf

1962: Gisela Kahn Gresser
1959: Lisa Lane
1957: Gisela Kahn Gresser - Sonja Graf
1955: Gisela Kahn Gresser - Nancy Roos
1953: Mona May Karff
1951: Mary Bain
1948: Gisela Kahn Gresser - Mona May Karff
1946: Mona May Karff
1944: Gisela Kahn Gresser
1942: Mona May Karff
1941: Mona May Karff
1940: Adele Rivero
1938: Mona May Karff
1937: Adele Rivero
Endnote [4]

Endnotes

[1] Tournament Announcement courtesy James Hodina, and www.iowachess.org

[2] http://chess.about.com/od/famouschessplayers/a/WorldChampions.htm

[3] www.uschess.org

[4] www.uschess.org

About the author

Ronn Munsterman is a Level I USCF Certified Coach with many years of coaching experience. His coaching philosophy is, first and foremost, that the game should be fun for the players and the coach. Known simply as "Coach," his students learn to play by all the rules of chess, learn sound chess fundamentals, and are challenged to grow stronger every week.

Munsterman joined the United States Chess Federation in 1987. He is a member of the Iowa State Chess Association and a Life Member of the Missouri Chess Association. He organized and ran the Kansas City Corporate Chess League from 1989 to 1991. From 1990 to 1995, Munsterman held several positions for the Missouri Chess Association, including member of the Board of Directors, President, Editor – *Missouri Chess Bulletin*, and Membership Coordinator.

In 1994, Munsterman won the Missouri State Reserve Championship with a score of 4.5 out of 5.

Munsterman began coaching when his son, Nathan, was in the first grade. He has coached players in grades 1 – 12. His elementary team from rural Troy, KS., won second place in two consecutive State championships, and one year won first place in six consecutive tournaments, all while competing against much larger schools. His players consistently placed in the top ten in Kansas Scholastic Chess Association tournaments, and won first place eight times. His top four players won the prestigious match-play Kansas City Cup twice, once in elementary, and once in middle school.

Munsterman currently coaches elementary and high school-aged players in Iowa where he lives with his wife, Berta.

17706702R00113

Made in the USA
Charleston, SC
24 February 2013